Praise for *An Economy of We...*

Economists often admit the many shortcomings ~~...~~ but then say, "however it is the best numerical proxy we have for unmeasurable welfare." Anielski demonstrates that there are other, better proxies, not to mention direct experience, common observation, and traditional wisdom. This is a book to be taken seriously."

— Herman Daly, Emeritus Professor,
School of Public Policy, University of Maryland

It's time we measured how organizations in all sectors are contributing to the five capitals that matter. Anielski shows how.

— Bob Willard, author, *The Sustainability Advantage*

One powerful answer to the struggling financial world around us. It very thoughtfully and clearly identifies how our existing debt and wealth measurement systems no longer serve our communities and our ability to live together in a just and balanced society. This is a great book, gracefully written, founded on doable optimism.

— Peter Block, author, *Flawless Consulting* and
co-author, *The Abundant Community*

Mark has been implementing happiness-creating economic system redesigns with towns, provinces, tribes, and nations. He has identified the major aspects of the current system that we must change to create a stable and happy society and what to do instead.

— Gifford Pinchot III, author, *Intrapreneuring*
and President Emeritus and Co-founder of the world's
first school with an MBA of Sustainable Business

Mark Anielski is one of those rare human beings who is equally at home with First Nation peoples of North America as he is with European Canadians, with the indigenous people of Bhutan, as he is with the Chinese and the Tahitians. As such, his work is uniquely all encompassing, a gift to those many worlds of which he is able to take integral account.

—Ronnie Lessem, Co-Founder, Trans4m Centre for Integral Development,
and Professor of Management, Da Vinci Institute

Mark Anielski has written a book that will, if attention is paid, open a new era in economics that will emancipate us from the lose-lose calculus of our current reasoning. His argument is compelling, rooted as it is in lived social reality.

— Walter Brueggemann, Professor of Theology,
Columbia Theological Seminary

You hold in your hand a rare synthesis between the deep understanding of the workings of our economy and a pragmatic methodology of implementation and integration towards a systemic well-being economy.

— Robert Dellner, Head of Impact & Strategy at Lintel Capital,
Co-Founder of the Centre for Integral Finance & Economics (CIFE)

A 21st century manifesto that addresses the problem of economic inequality. Those who turn to Anielski will find the rationale for demanding change in the relationship between government and its citizens back to its original intent—government that utilizes its economic tools to build an economy of well-being for its citizens.

— Luke Eckblad, Investment Banker, Boustead Institute

This book redefines what we mean by "The Wealth of Nations." It is a wonderful guide for people who want to take a path away from the monetization of everyday life.

— John McKnight, co-author, *The Abundant Community*,
and author, *The Careless Society*

Anielski has been a leading innovator on the cutting edge of well-being studies for three decades. I have been recommending Mark's work to people for decades, and now have another book to suggest.

— Marilyn Waring, Professor, Auckland University
and author, *If Women Counted*

Mark Anielski calls us to radically realign our economics with our anthropology, gives us a toolkit and the metrics to do so, and demonstrates different possible outcomes through concrete case studies.

— Seng-Kong Tan, Biblical Graduate School
of Theology, Singapore

Millard Fuller, the founder of Habitat for Humanity, would have applauded Mark Anielski for writing this book. Building a world of hope, where neighbours help neighbours, is to look beyond monetary profit.

— Alfred Nikolai, CEO of Habitat for Humanity,
Edmonton, Alberta, Canada

Like a pamphleteer of old, Anielski pushes into your hands a challenge to the existing system with a bold proposal of how it can be changed.

— Ian Glassford, Chief Financial Officer, Servus Credit Union

An Economy of Well-Being

COMMON-SENSE TOOLS *for* BUILDING
Genuine Wealth *and* Happiness

Mark Anielski

new society
PUBLISHERS

Cover design by Diane McIntosh.
Cover images © iStock.
Page 1 © Oleg Iatsun / Adobe Stock.

Printed in Canada. First printing May, 2018.

Inquiries regarding requests to reprint all or part of *An Economy of Well-Being* should be addressed to New Society Publishers at the address below. To order directly from the publishers, please call toll-free (North America) 1-800-567-6772, or order online at www.newsociety.com.

Any other inquiries can be directed by mail to

New Society Publishers
P.O. Box 189, Gabriola Island, BC V0R 1X0, Canada
(250) 247-9737

LIBRARY AND ARCHIVES CANADA CATALOGUING IN PUBLICATION

Anielski, Mark, 1960– , author
An economy of well-being : common-sense tools for building genuine wealth and happiness / Mark Anielski.

Includes index.
Issued in print and electronic formats.
ISBN 978-0-86571-873-9 (softcover).—ISBN 978-1-55092-666-8 (PDF).—
ISBN 978-1-77142-261-1 (EPUB)

1. Economics—Psychological aspects. 2. Well-being—Economic aspects.
3. Happiness—Economic aspects. 4. Wealth. I. Title.

HC26.A646 2018   330.01'9   C2018-900783-4
C2018-900784-2

Funded by the Government of Canada Financé par le gouvernement du Canada | Canadä

New Society Publishers' mission is to publish books that contribute in fundamental ways to building an ecologically sustainable and just society, and to do so with the least possible impact on the environment, in a manner that models this vision.

To Jennifer, Renee, Stephanie, Mary Ann and Jane,
who teach me humility

To my many friends around the world
who fill my life with joy

Contents

Figures

Tables

Foreword

by John Cobb Jr.

I thought I had a good general idea of where we "reformers" stood in relation to the actual functioning and control of the economy. My picture of the situation tended toward being depressing. This book shows me that I was ignorant. Far more change is happening in thought and in action than I recognized. The idea of establishing the goal of an economy of well-being is still marginal, but the margin is widening so rapidly that I am almost persuaded that we are close to a tilting point.

I am not an historian of these matters, so I will share instead my personal odyssey, believing that others have experienced the situation in similar ways. Until I was awakened to the global ecological crisis, I paid little attention to economics. The economy and the academic theory that supported it were givens to which I needed to adjust. But in the late '60s it became clear that economic considerations determined most national policy and that the policies they led to were running counter to the sustainability of life on the planet. I then worked with a few others to find ideas that took account of the seriousness of the crisis and yet proposed positive action. In economics, we were excited to come across the writings of Herman Daly. They were just what we hoped for. We featured him at our conference on "Alternatives to Catastrophe" in 1972. He has been my guide in economics ever since. We contributed essays to each other's edited books.

In the mid-'80s, we decided to write a book together. It was published as *For the Common Good* in 1989. It proposed an alternative to mainstream economics that would give major attention to the well-being of human communities, recognizing that they involve patterns of interpersonal relations of great importance to their members but are not considered in the mainstream theory or in government policies. It also emphasized the importance of the natural world and its well-being to human well-being.

As the book approached completion, I was troubled that we were not including a chapter on money. I, certainly, could not contribute much on that topic, but I assumed that this was a central topic among economists. I was shocked when Daly told me that there was little discussion of the nature or creation of money in standard economics. He said no one knows what money is.

A few years later, we agreed to publish an updated version. I pushed Daly hard to write about money, and you will find an appendix on this topic. Actually, I am proud of pressing him to do this. It is my impression that what he wrote there has helped to generate a discussion that by now has changed the situation. For many people now, money is not a mystery. Daly correctly identified it as debt created by banks when they make loans. At first, even saying this felt a bit daring. Now the Bank of England has confirmed it.

We agree today that the economy has shifted from being an industrial capitalism to a financial one. That makes an understanding of money even more important. In an industrial capitalism, banks made money by lending it, especially for the creation and expansion of factories and communications. In the process, production was increased. In financial capitalism, money is made by trading in different forms of money and by lending money for the purchase of money in ways that become more and more complex. Nothing of use to the public is produced. But wealth is concentrated more and more in the financial institutions and those who own or manage them.

As wealth is concentrated, so is power. Banks have always been powerful. But I doubt that any society in the past was as subservient to its financial institutions as ours is. If we were as ignorant of how money is created now as we were in the mid-'80s, we might just suppose that there is no alternative. But now that the literature on the subject is considerable, and the basic truth that money is created by banks by lending is undeniable, it is possible to affirm alternatives. I strongly recommend Chapter 10 of this book.

It explains that governments can establish banks that free them from interest payments and enable them to make money available to citizens at low borrowing costs. I share Anielski's enthusiasm for public banking as a cornerstone of economics for well-being.

There is now a significant movement in the United States for state banks. One, the Bank of North Dakota, has existed and benefited that state for decades. I have hoped that many other states would follow suit. But I have also been doubtful. These banks would break the monopoly of money creation by private finance, and in the long run they would reduce both its wealth and its power. My perception is that, thus far, financial interests have been able to block moves in many states to consider creating public banks. There seems a bit more hope for cities, but I am not sure that any of them can threaten the private monopoly. I have assumed that the control of the national government by Wall Street (and especially by Goldman Sachs) is such that change at the national level is currently impossible.

Anielski writes in a far more optimistic vein. Almost he persuades me, and, in any case, we should not give up without persistent trying. He is Canadian, and his province of Alberta, like North Dakota, has a flourishing public bank. For many years the national government of Canada had its own bank and, therefore, very little debt and great ability to fund the health and welfare of its people. Perhaps restoring that will not prove as difficult as would be the US treasury taking over the functions of the Federal Reserve in the United States. In any case, in both countries, despite the silence of the media, more and more people now understand how their lives could be dramatically improved by public banks.

With Daly's advice, a group of us in Claremont took up another project. We were appalled that so many political decisions are made with the goal of increasing GNP or GDP, both of which only measure market activity. Nations and international development agencies typically sought to increase gross domestic product. This meant that it was viewed as pure gain when a woman got a paying job and paid others to do housework and childcare. If that necessitated eating more at restaurants and buying a second car, so much the better. That all adds to GDP. No question is asked about whether the family is really better off economically, much less whether its members are happier.

Consider another feature. If an earthquake destroys much of a city, nothing is subtracted from GDP. On the contrary, the GDP is benefited by all the work required for rebuilding. Even if the city is permanently impoverished by the disaster, it is considered to have made great progress. A country that is rapidly exhausting its natural resources, such as forests and oil, may have a high GDP, but even some economists have noted that unless this wealth is invested in productive ways, this is not good for the people.

Our group proposed a measure that took account of these absurdities. We called it the Index of Sustainable Economic Welfare (ISEW). We thought that since we developed it without challenging standard economic theory, economists might welcome it. But they did not. It has been further developed as the Genuine Progress Indicator to which Anielski makes reference, but still without seeming to have any effect on the recommendations of economists. I have been discouraged.

However, much of Anielski's book describes changes in the situation of which I was unaware. The need for better measures is far more widely recognized now than when we worked on the ISEW. Furthermore, many of the proposals that are now taken seriously go far beyond ours. We thought that there was no chance of getting a measure accepted that was not strictly focused on economic considerations readily measured in dollars. But now there has been remarkable progress in defining happiness or well-being in terms that can be measured. Furthermore, many agree that the economy should not aim primarily at its own growth, even when this is measured more realistically, but at the well-being of the people. Anielski shows that there are not only efforts to measure this but political efforts to seek this end. To my astonishment and delight he opens my eyes to the rapidity with which progress toward an economy of well-being is being recognized as the proper goal and has even been adopted.

Anielski is not ignorant of the powers arrayed against the widespread adoption of this goal and of the banking system that would make progress achievable. But this is not a book about obstacles. It is a book about the progress that has been made and is now being made. Anielski shows us a movement worthy of our support, even of our personal sacrifice. He shows us that it is not utopian in a negative sense. Its goals are realizable. Throw out the old saw that "there is no alternative." There *is* an alternative, and this is it, or better, this is an indispensable and foundational feature of the alternative.

Spread the word that we do not have to serve the banks. We can have banks that serve us. Once we really understand the money whose concentration gives such excessive power to those who create it, we can together declare independence and make our own. Then, if we have the will and wisdom, we can adopt policies that will make for the sustainable well-being of the biosphere, with special attention to humanity. MAY IT BE SO!

JOHN B. COBB, Jr. is an American philosopher, theologian, and environmentalist and is often cited as one of the most important North American theologians of the 20th century. He is the preeminent scholar in the school of thought associated with the philosophy of Alfred North Whitehead. The author of more than 50 books, Cobb is a member of the American Academy of Arts and Sciences—one of the nation's highest honors.

Introduction:
A New Economic Paradigm
Based on Well-Being

THIS BOOK REPRESENTS my vision for a new economic paradigm that would place well-being at the heart of all economic and monetary policies and make well-being the highest aspiration of businesses, communities and nations.

The dominant era of financial capitalism is waning. There is a hunger for a new economic paradigm and model that aligns with a common yearning for a life of meaning, sufficient income for material needs, as well as a life of meaning and joy.

Various economic authors have begun to identify some of the key shortcomings of modern economic systems—for example, Thomas Piketty, author of *Capital in the Twenty-First Century* (2015), whom some critics have hailed as a modern "Marx" for revealing the negative impacts of inequality of income and wealth since the industrial revolution. Others have offered a new economic vision, such as David Korten in his most recent work, *Agenda for a New Economy: From Phantom Wealth to Real Wealth* (2010). Most either provide either a depressing prognosis of the economic patient or offer inadequate and often impractical alternatives to the dominant system of financial capitalism.

Some economists, including ecological economists (Peter Victor, Herman Daly and others), go beyond constant economic growth, suggesting zero-growth and steady-state economics as a solution to pressing issues such as climate change. Yet most fail to identify what I believe is the hidden cancer that threatens to kill most world economies: unsustainable levels of exponential, bank-created debt. Economists Graeme Maxton and Jorgen Sanders, in their new book *Reinventing Prosperity: Managing Economic Growth to Reduce Unemployment, Inequality and Climate Change* (2016), provide what they believe are politically viable solutions to some of the most pressing challenges of our time, including rising income inequality, climate change and the replacement of human labor with robots. Yet I find these proposals lacking in practical common-sense attributes that would transition our economies from a current state of economic cancer to ones that are truly flourishing and resilient. Most economists demonstrate a fundamental lack of understanding of how the current debt-money system works, which is, in my opinion, the most important issue preventing our economies and our own economic lives from achieving genuine happiness.

Ironically, while many of these economists anticipate that policy advisers and decision-makers may find hope in their proposed solutions, many, like Maxton and Sanders, seem resigned to a dark future in which their list of solutions may have absolutely no chance of being accepted by those in power—financiers, the rich and big corporations. Instead, they hope that people will read their book, recognize the benefits and feel compelled to vote in democratic elections for the party that would courageously present their new economic agenda.

The economy of well-being model I propose will hopefully have the greatest chance of success, primarily because it is built on the best attributes of economics and accounting from the past five hundred years while shifting the focus of economic policies from pure economic growth and debt-based monetary policies to one of economic, social and environmental well-being. This would return economics to its Greek origins, namely, what Aristotle called *oikos-nomia*, meaning good "household management." Moreover, it would revisit Adam Smith's *Wealth of Nations* through the original Old English definition of wealth (*wela-th*), meaning "the conditions of well-being." Had Smith used this original definition of wealth, his seminal book from 1776 would have been titled *The Well-Being of Nations*. Well-being can be defined as people's own positive evaluations of their lives, which include positive emotions (happiness), engagement (relationships), life satisfaction and meaning (Seligman, 2002).[1]

Imagine if the fields of economics, accounting and finance in the United States, Canada, Europe and Asia had focused on well-being rather than the primacy of financial capital and economic growth. The premise of my work is to make well-being the primary focus of policy makers in government, communities, business and the world of finance and money. This would mean a shift in economic theory and policy toward the wise stewardship and well-being of both the households and communities that make up nations, in harmony with the resilience of Mother Nature.

I will attempt to lay out a clear architecture and road map for building the new economy of well-being, which I believe to be more compelling than the current economic paradigms. I believe well-being economics will appeal to a broad spectrum of political and spiritual ideologies and beliefs. I offer it as a model for a moderate and middle path for any community, state, province or nation.

Abrahm Maslow defined a hierarchy of needs; at the peak of his hierarchy was self-actualization, spiritual fulfillment and happiness. But he defined happiness in the original Greek—*Eudaimonia*, meaning "the well-being of spirit." Maslow, like Aristotle, understood that the highest aspiration of the human being was to achieve their full potential or vocation. I believe Maslow, like the Indigenous people of North America who inspired his model, would agree that human flourishing and well-being (physical, mental, emotional and spiritual) is the ultimate aspiration of all people.

This common-sense economic evolution will require a fundamental restructuring of our money systems, which have been dominated by a debt-money system that emerged from London in

1694 with the founding of the Bank of England. Few economists understand how the debt-money system of private bank-created financial capital works and that it is the key driver behind an obsession with economic growth. The human and environmental costs (in the form of interest cost of debt money) of this brilliant system of fractional reserve banking is the elephant in the room of economic forums such as the World Economic Forum. Why is this never discussed in *The Economist* or at G7/G20 or other forums dealing with public policy?

In an economy of well-being, money and its creation would be governed collectively to contribute to the greatest good of all people. This shift in our economic consciousness from casino capitalism, individualism and materialism to well-being is not as difficult as some might think. It would entail working within the existing tools and practices of economics, accounting and finance but with a new perspective that would focus on the highest and best use of assets.

Economic and monetary policies and models would seek to find well-being optimization of the total assets of a state or nation. This would require a cross-disciplinary approach to economic well-being analysis and an expansion of modern accounting practices to account for a broader suite of assets (human, social and natural capital), using well-being impact indicators and a well-being bottom line to assess the long-term sustainability of businesses, enterprises and government organizations. The purpose of business and finance would become "doing well by doing good."

Since my first book, *The Economics of Happiness: Building Genuine Wealth*, was published by New Society in 2007, I have promoted the ideas and tools for this new economy of well-being in Canada, the United States, China, Bhutan, England, the Netherlands, Austria, Tahiti, the Vatican and several First Nations (Indigenous communities) in Canada. Many political leaders are intrigued with the ideas but naturally ask, "Where has this been applied successfully before?" Like any paradigm shift, it is in the trials, tribulations, successes and failures that the practical aspects of this new economic model emerge. This book contains some of the stories about my experiences, whether at a large, national scale as in China or in a small First Nation community of three hundred in Canada.

One of my favorite stories is the first time I had a chance to pitch the economy of well-being concept to the World Economic Forum, in 2011. This forum is held every year in Davos, Switzerland, and brings together the world's leading economic thinkers, politicians and business people. My friend and colleague Toby Heaps (CEO of Corporate Knights Inc. and Clean Capitalism) called me one evening in January 2011 from Toronto's Pearson International Airport. He told me that he was co-hosting a dinner gala at the Forum and asked if I could prepare a short ideas paper on natural capital and the economics of well-being for billionaire George Soros, Deutsche Bank vice-chairman Ciao Koch-Weser and Jim Balsillie, then CEO of Research in Motion (RIM), makers of Blackberry. My proposal encouraged Soros and Koch-Weser to consider a new economic paradigm and financial architecture based on an integrated genuine wealth model focused on well-being. I reasoned that several nations and communities were already making prudent steps toward developing well-being indicator systems, building economies of well-being and focusing on happiness as an objective of economic development.

Soros, a shrewd financial capitalist, currency trader and philanthropist, responded to my proposal with the following words: "I am on board with the fundamental importance of the genuine wealth idea, but there is a lack of sentiment that a framework for more holistic wealth is ready for prime time." Deutsche Bank's Caio Koch-Weser was intrigued with the ideas and offered to be a "sherpa" of a focused set of material placed in the right political hands at the forthcoming G20 summit. Five years have now passed since he encouraged me to prepare a road map to a new economic future. This book is that road map.

In a letter to his grandchildren, British economist John Maynard Keynes (who gave the world Keynesian economics and GDP accounting during the time of the Great Depression) expressed a compelling vision for our economic future. He noted that he saw a future in which we would once again ponder the real meaning of virtue:

> I see us free, therefore, to return to some of the most sure and certain principles of religion and traditional virtue—that avarice is a vice, that the exaction of usury is a misdemeanor, and the love of money is detestable, that those walk most truly in the paths of virtue and sane wisdom who take least thought for the morrow. We shall once more value ends above means and prefer the good to the useful. We shall honour those who can teach us how to pluck the hour and the day virtuously and well, the delightful people who are capable of taking direct enjoyment in things, the lilies of the field who toil not, neither do they spin.[2]

What would Keynes offer the world today—a world of chronic and unsustainable levels of financial debts which can never be repaid? How would he respond to my proposal that a more stable and resilient economic future can be secured by ensuring that the true wealth and assets of all nations are wisely managed to achieve the highest possible well-being outcomes for the greatest number of human beings?

Moreover, can the creation of money be aligned with the goals of the highest and best use of the aggregate assets of nations for maximizing a well-being return on investment, without the unnecessary and hidden burden of compound interest on debt-money? What if money creation and monetary policies were linked to the goals of improving well-being? Could money be created by public banks backed 100% by the real and verifiable assets of our communities, thereby alleviating the high cost of compound interest hidden in the current debt-money economy? How would a new financial system operate if it were based on maximizing well-being rather than simply GDP or financial profits? How would we measure progress in terms of the conditions of well-being in our communities and in the natural environment?

The financial crisis of 2008 revealed the vulnerability of the world's financial system to near collapse. In 2017 the world's economy is even more unstable as total outstanding debts rise exponentially. Big New York-based banks (too big to fail) were bailed out with trillions of new debt money that now exacts an even higher and hidden toll on average American households. US Federal Reserve statistics reveal that the average American household earning $55,000 will spend roughly half of their income on interest costs hidden in the prices of all goods and services; these compound interest costs are the result of a total US debt load of $66 trillion, which grows exponentially. Meanwhile, real household incomes remain stagnant, many live paycheck-to-paycheck, financial wealth is concentrated in fewer pockets, overall self-rated happiness declines, many youth and low-income and middle-class American households despair about their future, and the overall conditions of well-being for millions continue to fall.

Is there a way out of this economic straitjacket? Is there a cure to what appears to be the cancer state of financial capitalism?

This book is meant to engender hope that a dark age ahead can be avoided and the current system of economic malaise transcended with a more compelling economic future based on the goal of well-being. Follow me to discover the geography of economic hope from New York to London, from Shanghai to the Hague, from rural Alberta to the paradise island of Tahiti and the ancient longhouse of the Onondaga Iroquois Nation in upstate New York. Learn why I believe the Iroquois matrilineal hereditary governance structure and wampum (shell-based money system) that inspired George Washington and Benjamin Franklin to envision the United States of America might again be the spark of a new economy. Learn how the tiny Buddhist Kingdom of Bhutan is adopting the Gross National Happiness measure of progress and how many Canadian communities are adopting a new Index of Well-Being. Learn how a new generation of impact investment bankers and modern public banks are reinventing the world of finance and banking and creating a new financial architecture that could underpin the economy of well-being and solve some of the world's most longstanding challenges, such as poverty and climate change. May these examples and ideas for building a new economy of well-being bring the world hope.

Notes

1. M. E. P. Seligman. *Authentic happiness: Using the new positive psychology to realize your potential for lasting fulfillment.* New York: Free Press, 2002.
2. John Maynard Keynes. "Economic Possibilities for our Grandchildren." John Maynard Keynes, *Essays in Persuasion*, New York: W. W. Norton, 1963, pp. 358–373.

CHAPTER 1

Reclaiming Economics for Happiness

Happiness is the meaning and the purpose of life,
the whole aim and end of human existence.
— Aristotle

One must make a new system
that makes the old system obsolete.
— Buckminster Fuller

Reclaiming the Language of Economics

Economics and the gospel of economic growth have failed humanity when it comes to delivering the well-being we all desire: to live happy and meaningful lives. The economics of eternal growth has lost touch with the original Greek meaning of the word economy (*oikonomia*), which referred to the wise management of the household. Instead, genuine economics—a concern for the well-being of the household—has been usurped by a culture of hedonistic materialism and love of money. Aristotle argued that *chrematistics*—the art of getting rich, or the science of making and accumulating money—was an unnatural activity that dehumanized those who practiced it. He condemned the practice of making money from money, stating unequivocally, "The trade of the petty usurer is hated with most reason: it makes a profit from currency itself, instead of making it from the process which currency was meant to serve. Their common characteristic is obviously their sordid avarice."

While the word *usury* seems to have faded from the consciousness of modern times, Pope Francis seems to agree with Aristotle
and the 14th-century theologian Thomas Aquinas[1] in condemn-
ing it:

> I hope that these institutions may intensify their commit-
> ment alongside the victims of usury, a dramatic social ill.
> When a family has nothing to eat, because it has to make
> payments to usurers, this is not Christian, it is not human!
> This dramatic scourge in our society harms the inviolable
> dignity of the human person.[2]

Today modern usury happens whenever private banks make
new loans, creating new money (*ex nihilo*: out of nothing) as
simple bookkeeping entries in their ledgers unattached to real
assets. The costs to all of society are the interest charges on each
loan. The totality of all loans created primarily by private banks
in every economy constitutes the total debt-money supply of
nations.

Returning the world to the original vision of economics as the
Greeks defined it will require a serious examination by economists of the evidence that usury—the creation of money as debt
and the charging of interest—has indeed decimated the well-
being of millions of households and made the pursuit of genuine
happiness difficult, at best.

As an adjunct professor of corporate social responsibility and
social entrepreneurship at the University of Alberta's School of
Business, I would ask my business students, What is an economy
for? What is the real purpose and role of business in an economy?
What is the role and responsibility of business in a society focused on returns to well-being? Why do we measure progress the
way we do? Why is it that despite rising levels of gross domestic
product (GDP), we have diminishing levels of self-rated happiness
in the US, as well as the erosion of many well-being conditions?
If the promise of a rising tide of continuous economic growth
was to lift the prospects of every American household, why has
it failed to do so in the land that espouses the pursuit of happiness as its highest aspiration? How is it that governments operate

without a complete balance sheet that shows the assets and liabilities of the human, social, natural and built assets of the state
or nation? What if the progress of our economies were measured
in terms of the conditions of well-being and self-rated happiness
that psychologists tell us contribute most to our genuine happiness and societal well-being, including the strength and joy of our
relationships?

Happiness: Well-Being of Spirit

It is worth repeating that Aristotle defined the word *happiness* in
terms of the Greek work *eudaimonia*, which translates literally into
"good spirit." Another translation is "human flourishing" or "the
good life."[3] I would define happiness as "the well-being of one's
spirit or soul." The Oxford Dictionary defines well-being as "the
state of being comfortable, healthy, or happy." Happiness is much
more than a pleasant or contented mental state. Happiness is a
mental or emotional state of well-being that can be defined and
measured as a range of emotions from contentment to intense
joy. Joy itself is perhaps the ultimate aspiration—a state of bliss.
Aristotle said that happiness results from a good birth, accompa-
nied by a lifetime of good friends, good children, health, wealth, a
contented old age and virtuous activity. The Buddha agreed with
Aristotle that the purpose of our lives is to be happy.

Ultimately, Aristotle defined *eudaimonia* as the rational activity of the soul in accordance with virtue in a complete life. It
is the basis of Aristotle's ethical and political theory, the goal of
all action, which can be attained through virtue. For this reason,
Aristotle's ethics and politics were heavily focused on virtue.[4] This
was also true of Benjamin Franklin and Thomas Jefferson; Jefferson noted that without virtue one cannot be happy.

Imagine if Thomas Jefferson, who penned the US *Declaration
of Independence*, had replaced the word *happiness* with *well-being*,
as follows: "We hold these truths to be self-evident; that all men
and women are created equal and independent, that from that
equal creation they derive rights inherent and inalienable, among
which are the preservation of a good life, and liberty, and the pursuit of well-being."[5]

What has become of virtue in our modern *politikos*? How would the US measure its progress through this new aspirational lens of well-being, including both spiritual and other aspects of well-being and a good life?

A New Index of Well-Being

Since the 1970s, some progressive economists (along with Robert Kennedy in 1968) have been advocating for a new economic measure of welfare to either replace or modify GDP and national income accounts with a new measure or index of progress. It wasn't until 1996 that the San Francisco-based economic think tank Redefining Progress produced a new measure of sustainable economic well-being, which they called the Genuine Progress Indicator (GPI). The GPI was inspired by the seminal 1989 work *For the Common Good* by Dr. John Cobb Jr. (one of the two most important American theologians of the 20th century, from Claremont School of Theology in California) and Dr. Herman Daly (an ecological economist and advocate for a steady-state economy from the University of Maryland).[6]

In 2004 positive psychologists Dr. Ed Diener (University of Illinois) and Dr. Martin Seligman (University of Pennsylvania) proposed the development of a national well-being accounting system and index for the United States. This system of well-being accounts would systemically assess key variables of well-being such as trust, belonging, engagement, meaning and life satisfaction. This would be a subjective well-being index based on the perceptions of Americans. However, to date no such national well-being accounting system or index has been adopted by the US or any US state or city, with a few exceptions, including the city of Santa Monica, California, which has adopted a Wellbeing Index to measure and actively improve the state of the community.[7]

Nonetheless, the US Gallup-Healthways Well-Being Index, which claims to be the "Dow Jones of Health," is produced daily. The Index tracks well-being aspects of the lives of a sample of 1,000 Americans each day. The methodology underlying it uses the World Health Organization's definition of health as "not only the absence of infirmity and disease, but also a state of physical, mental, and social wellbeing."[8] The Well-Being Index includes citizen self-ratings of economic confidence, work satisfaction, overall happiness, hope and other variables. While Gallup-Healthways reports on state-level well-being, there is still no national well-being index we might contrast with changes in the US GDP.

The happiest state in the union is consistently Hawaii, which, according to Gallup-Healthways, reached the top spot once more in 2015, for the fifth time since they began tracking well-being in 2008. Alaska is typically ranked second, while West Virginia and Kentucky consistently rank the lowest and second-lowest in well-being nationally.

One of the more interesting trends involves Americans' perceptions of their standard of living (is it getting better or worse?) and whether they feel their economic future is bright or dark. The graph suggests that a growing number of Americans feel satisfied with their current standard of living and are more hopeful about their economic future compared with 2008, the year of the financial crisis.

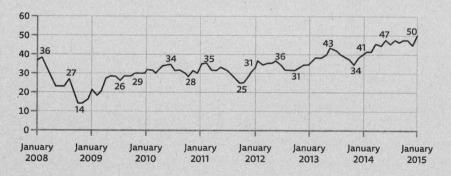

1   **Gallup US Standard of Living Index, Monthly Averages**

The Standard of Living Index is based on a composite of these two questions:

1. Right now, do you feel your standard of living is getting better or getting worse?

2. Are you satisfied with your standard of living, all the things you can buy and do?

SOURCE: gallup.com/poll/180449/standard-living-index-climbs-highest-years.aspx.

However, a different picture emerges in the United Kingdom. According to a UK Gallup poll, UK citizens' perceptions of "thriving" or happiness show a marked decline since the Brexit referendum vote of June 23, 2016, which led to the UK planning to leave the European Union. In the two years leading up to Brexit, Gallup found that the percentage of people who were "happy" (or "thriving") was already in dramatic decline. In fact, the 15-percentage-point decline in the percentage of people rating their lives positively enough to be considered thriving was so dramatic it remains among the largest two-year drops in Gallup's history of global tracking.[9] This was in spite of a 2% increase in the country's gross domestic product and a relatively low unemployment rate of 4.9%.

In the United States, levels of happiness have been in decline since the early 1950s, when the first happiness polls were taken. The levels of very happy and happy people reached a near recorded low in 2016, with only 31% of American's feeling very happy compared with 53% in the early 1950s (see Figure 3).[10] Yet at the same time, real (inflation-adjusted) GDP per capita has continued to rise.

The Harris Poll® Happiness Index,[11] which uses a series of questions to calculate Americans' overall happiness, found that in 2016, fewer than one in three Americans (31%) were very happy,

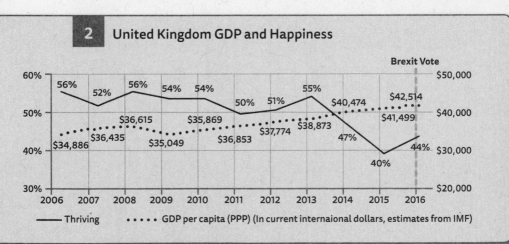

2 United Kingdom GDP and Happiness

SOURCE: Gallup World Poll and UK GDP statistics.

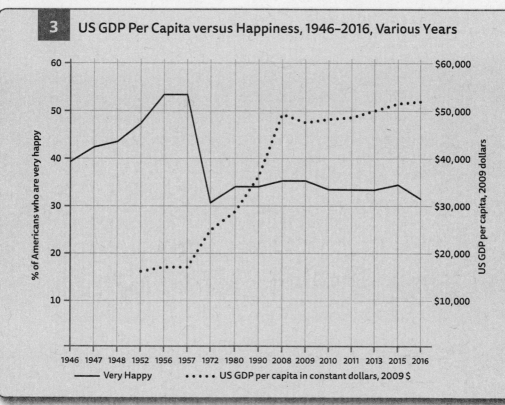

3 US GDP Per Capita versus Happiness, 1946–2016, Various Years

— Very Happy   ····· US GDP per capita in constant dollars, 2009 $

SOURCE: Data for US happiness is from the Harris Happiness Index Poll 2008–2016. Previous happiness survey results are from various sources including Oswald J. Andrew, "Happiness and Economic Performance." The Economic Journal, 107, November 1997, 1815–1831. US GDP per capita is from the US Bureau of Economic Analysis data.

down from just over one in three (34%) in 2015. At the same time, however, about eight in ten US adults (81%) say they are generally happy with their life right now, suggesting that people may overstate how happy they really are.

Kathy Steinberg, managing editor of the Harris Poll, points out that as part of the survey, pollsters don't ask "Why do you feel this way?" or "What has changed?" But the numbers do show that certain groups of people are happier. For example, women tend to be happier than men. People with annual income between $50,000 and $74,999 are actually happier overall than people who earn between $75,000 and $99,999. People with a college degree are happier than those without. African-Americans tend to be slightly happier than Whites and Whites happier than Hispanics. Seniors (people 65 and up) are the happiest age group, and married people are happier than unmarried people. Having a child under the age of eighteen has no statistical impact on happiness, while people who live in the suburbs are happier than others. However, Steinberg cautions interpreting these happiness results. The Happiness Index, she notes, reveals the "general principle that people self-report that they're happier than they may actually be."[12]

Measuring Well-Being Objectively

What about a measure of objective well-being? New measures of progress, including the Genuine Progress Indicator and the Canadian Index of Wellbeing (CIW), have emerged in the past ten years. I will discuss the CIW later in the book; a 64-indicator objective index of well-being, inspired, in part, by the earlier work on the GPI.

The US GPI provided a reasonable response to Bobby Kennedy's 1968 challenge to the GDP (Gross Domestic Product)—that it needed to be revised to measure the economic activities that actually contributed to a good life and to well-being, instead of simply measuring the amount of money exchanging hands in the economy. It was developed by economists to provide a broad measure of economic well-being that could be compared with GDP and other traditional economic indicators. The GPI measures the overall well-being of a nation, while the GDP measures only the money value of all economic output, or production of the economy. It starts with GDP (the gross value of all goods and services produced/consumed in an economy), then subtracts harmful things like crime, pollution, illness, loss of farmland and wetlands, declining water quality and the negative impact of income inequality. It also adds the unaccounted and non-money value of unpaid work in the home and volunteering in the community (see Figure 4).

The US GPI-GDP graph (Figure 5) clearly shows that economic well-being peaked in the United States about the time of the OPEC oil crisis in 1973. The two-year period that followed (1973–75) was

4 The Genuine Progress Indicator: Indicators of Well-Being

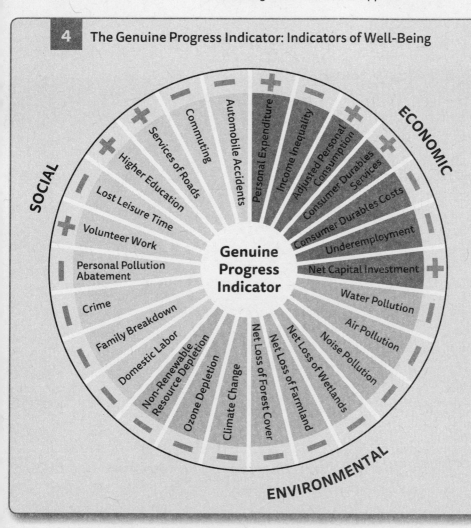

a formative tipping point for the US and other world economies. In 1971 President Richard Nixon unilaterally cancelled the direct convertibility of the US dollar to gold. Without a gold standard to temper debt-money and economic growth, there was a surge in private-bank-created debt money (see Chapter 10). For example, the ratio of US total *debt to GDP* between 1950 and 1971 averaged between 129% and 151%; as I write this (October 2017), it now stands at 364% and continues to climb.[13] Interest costs embedded in the economy are a significant (although unaccounted

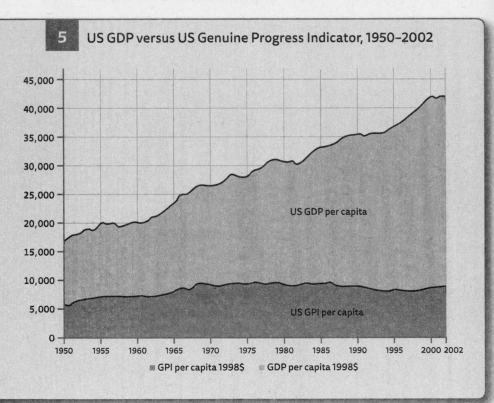

5 US GDP versus US Genuine Progress Indicator, 1950–2002

GPI per capita 1998$ GDP per capita 1998$

SOURCE: Redefining Progress, Oakland, California.

for) contributor to US GDP and the second-largest expense item (though not fully accounted for) in the US federal government budget, higher than defense and second only to health care.[14] The burden of interest costs associated with debt-money is cutting off the oxygen of the US economy and American households.

It appears that 1974–76 was a key tipping point for the United States in terms of a number of well-being conditions; this was also true of other nations. The US GPI peaked in 1976 and had declined 7.7% by 2002 (the last time the GPI was updated), despite a 71% increase in real (inflation-adjusted) GDP per capita. What happened at this key juncture in US history? The GPI provides a clue. Many factors—including income inequality and environmental and social costs related to economic progress—have been rising faster than the consumption-based GDP. In addition, soaring interest rates and rising levels of both private and public debt are consuming ever-increasing amounts of households' disposable income and eroding the spending power of governments.

In the 2001 Alberta GPI project, a research project I led with the Pembina Institute, Canada's first well-being index showed trends in 50 indicators of well-being for the province of Alberta over a 40-year period (1961–2001). The results showed that the overall state of well-being in Alberta had declined overall since the early 1960s. There were some expectations—including higher life expectancies and rising household incomes—but key areas of diminished quality of life include rising income inequality and levels of household debt, increased levels of suicide and problem gambling, obesity, increases in the time required to earn a sufficient income and the greater ecological footprints of households. Similar to the US GPI, it seemed that the years 1973–74 represent a major tipping point in well-being. This was particularly strange since Alberta benefited from the OPEC oil crisis of 1973, riding a wave of rising oil prices thanks to its abundant oil and natural gas resources. These trends showed that the economists' belief that "a rising tide of economic growth (measured by GDP) would lift all economic boats" was not a reality for most Albertans.

While the GPI offers one of the best alternative measures of well-being to the GDP—and there have been recent attempts to adopt the GPI at the state (Maryland, Oregon, Vermont) and provincial levels (Alberta, Nova Scotia) and the Canadian Index of Wellbeing nationally—there remains no firm political commitment to adopt this common-sense alternative measure of progress, either in the United States or Canada.

Alberta's Economic Growth, Disease and Income Inequality

Two of the more disturbing statistics I have tracked since completing the Alberta GPI in 2001 are the correlation between the incidence of cancer and both GDP and income inequality. Between 1981 and 2016, the incidence of all cancers (the rate per 100,000 people) increased by 51.2% for both males and females. By comparison, Alberta's real per capita GDP increased by 28.7%

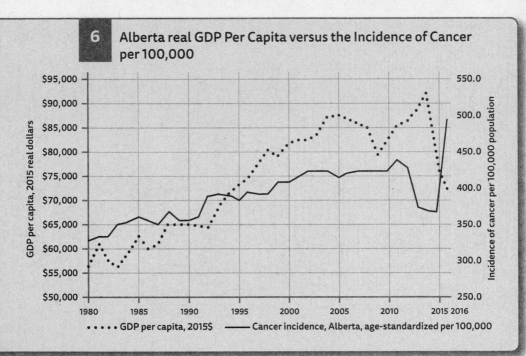

6 **Alberta real GDP Per Capita versus the Incidence of Cancer per 100,000**

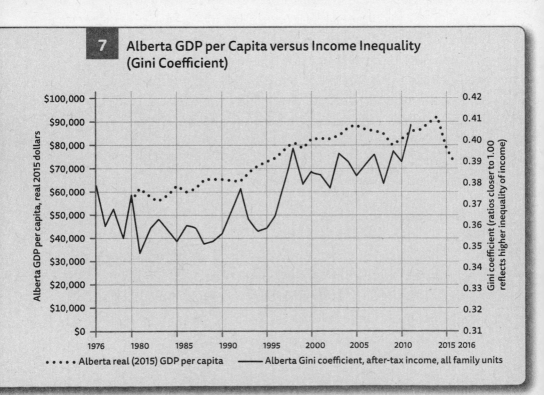

7 **Alberta GDP per Capita versus Income Inequality (Gini Coefficient)**

over the same period. Ironically, it seems that more cancer is good for Alberta's economy; indeed, the more people with cancer, the more we spend on cancer treatment, and the more GDP grows. Yet cancer brings considerable unhappiness to our lives, which is not measured in GDP terms.

Similar trends were found when comparing income inequality and GDP. Income inequality is a good measure of social capital or social cohesion: societies with less income inequality (using a measure called the Gini coefficient) tend to be happier, more trusting and more cohesive. According to Figure 7, income inequality has been rising since 1981 in Alberta, which is second only to British Columbia among Canadian provinces in terms of the gap between rich and poor. Alberta's Gini coefficient increased 9.1% between 1981 and 2011, while real GDP per capita (2015 dollars) increased 53.5%. The rise in income inequality was statistically correlated with GDP. Why is inequality important to happiness?

According to epidemiologists Richard Wilkinson and Kate Picket in *The Spirit Level: Why More Equal Societies Almost Always Do Better*, 2009, evidence shows that inequality in societies leads to regrettable erosion in social capital. The authors found that inequality causes shorter, unhealthier and unhappier lives; increases the rates of teenage pregnancy, violence, obesity, imprisonment and addiction; destroys relationships between individuals born in the same society but into different classes; and functions as a driver of consumption that depletes the planet's resources. They also show that for virtually every measure of quality of life there is a strong correlation between a country's level of economic inequality and its social outcomes. In almost all cases, Japan and the Scandinavian countries are at the favorable "low" end of inequality and the United Kingdom, the United States and Portugal are at the unfavorable "high" end, with Canada, Australasia and continental European countries in between. The bottom line is that societies tend to be happier when there is a more equal distribution of money, income and financial wealth.

Exposing the Myth of Productivity

Economists love to talk about the importance of the productivity of nations as a key measure of progress and success. Most of us have no idea what productivity is or how economists measure it. In simplified terms, productivity is measured as the ratio of economic output (GDP) to either the number of employed persons or the number of hours worked in the economy. The higher the GDP per capita the more successfully an economy is presumed to be performing. But what does productivity have to do with the well-being of individual workers, their workplace or their family well-being? How should we measure these attributes of work?

The following graph (Figure 8) shows the trends in US productivity, GDP per capita, wages and salaries per employee and the US Genuine Progress Index from 1960–2016. The graph shows how real GDP per capita (2009 dollars) has risen faster (210%)

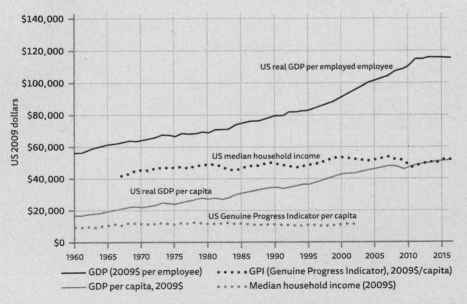

8 US Productivity (GDP Per Employee), GDP Per Capita, Salaries and Wages Per Employee and US Genuine Progress Indicator, Indexed 1960=100, Based on 2009 Real Dollars

SOURCE: Data from the US Bureau of Economic Analysis and Redefining Progress (San Francisco).

than productivity (GDP per employed workers in the US), which rose 106%. At the same time, average real (2009 dollars) median household income rose by only 25.5% between 1967 and 2015, from $41,452 per household in 1967 to $52,029 in 2015.[15] However a more complete well-being index, the US GPI, rose only 26% over the period 1960–2002, having peaked in the mid-1970s when real wages and full employment were highest.

Statistics thus show that real household income and overall well-being conditions for the average American have not kept pace with economic growth. They also show the value of measuring productivity and progress beyond simply GDP per worker, on a more meaningful basis of changes in the well-being conditions of households.

Measuring Happiness is All the Rage

Since the release of my first book in 2007, there has been an explosion of other books and works on the economics of happiness. In 2009, French President Nicolas Sarkozy formed a commission led by former World Bank chief economist and Nobel Prize winner Joseph Stiglitz, among others, to conceive of a new accounting system for measuring progress and well-being. Sarkozy urged other countries to adopt new measures of economic output, noting that the world has become trapped in a "cult of figures" and "behind the cult of figures, behind all these statistical and accounting structures, there is also the cult of the market that is always right." Sarkozy's commission reported that gross domestic product was flawed even as a measure of economic output, failing to account properly for public services or home-based activities. Worse, GDP was often equated with well-being itself and could also create perverse incentives. For example, it included spending on prisons and security systems, implying that more of this was good for society. Stiglitz noted that "what we measure affects what we do…. If we have the wrong measures, we will strive for the wrong things." The Stiglitz commission proposed the use of objective measures of well-being and subjective indicators of happiness, covering income and wealth, health, education, social connections and relationships, the environment, insecurity and even political systems.

In November 2010, British Prime Minister David Cameron announced that Great Britain would begin to measure happiness as an alternative and better measure of how the country was doing. Cameron noted that GDP, and thus national income, accounts were no longer up to the job. As part of the National Well-Being Project, the Office for National Statistics would ask citizens to rate their own well-being, including self-rated happiness, anxiety and feelings that life is worthwhile. The first official happiness index was released in 2012. According to Abbie Self, Director of Well-Being, Inequalities, Sustainability and Environment in the UK, the most recent index for 2015–16 showed that "Life satisfaction has increased over the past year, which is what one might expect given the improvements seen in the economy and record high employment during that period. However, what is more surprising is that there is no change over the same time in people's happiness, anxiety and feeling that what they do in life is worthwhile. This is the first time we haven't seen year-on-year improvements in these particular measures since we began collecting the data in 2011."[16]

In May of 2011, China's National People's Congress (NPC) announced that happiness is now more important to China's future than increasing GDP. A new five-year plan adopted at the meeting was hailed as a blueprint for a "happy China."

And in 2012, the tiny Buddhist Kingdom of Bhutan encouraged all nations of the world at the United Nations to adopt a new economic paradigm based on well-being and happiness.

The UN now produces an annual *World Happiness Report*. The fourth annual report of 2017 ranked 157 countries, with Norway (7.537), Denmark (7.522), Iceland (7.504), Switzerland (7.494) and Finland (7.469) making up the top five happiest nations. Canada ranked seventh overall, down one spot from 2015. The United States ranked 14th, the United Kingdom 19th, France 31st, Italy at 48th, Russia 49th and Bhutan (home of the Gross National Happiness index) 97th. Those who thought Bhutan would be the happiest nation on the planet might be surprised that life satisfaction is lower than we might expect; there is no logical explanation for why Nordic countries are happier than the Buddhist nation of Bhutan.

Happiness economists have found that the key factors that differentiate the top ten happiest nations from others include GDP per capita, social supports, healthy life expectancy, freedom, corruption and differences in generosity. Sufficient income (measured in terms of GDP) does matter to a certain level of subjective happiness, but beyond that it is social factors, including healthy relationships, trust and reciprocity, which add to marginal happiness.

According to economist Jeffrey Sachs, one of the co-authors of the *World Happiness Report* along with Canadian economist John Helliwell (University of British Columbia) and Richard Layard (Columbia University), the report aims to measure "the scientific underpinnings of subjective well-being." Sachs and Helliwell believe it is possible to orient public policy, economic development goals and budgets toward well-being rather than focusing uniquely on maximizing GDP and productivity. I agree and suggest that an even broader suite of well-being and progress indicators be incorporated into governance and budgeting systems for municipalities, states/provinces and nations.

People Prefer Happiness over Wealth

In polls conducted by Gallup, most people around the world rate happiness above material wealth and even health. Positive psychologist Ed Diener found that in the 2010 Gallup poll results for 28 countries, including the United States, China, Hong Kong, Japan and Singapore, happiness was rated most important (8.0 average on a scale of 1 to 9), over wealth (6.8) and slightly higher than health (7.9).[17] This suggests that for most of us, personal happiness remains our highest individual and collective aspiration.

According to Diener's research, there is less of a correlation between income and levels of happiness and life satisfaction. He compares South Korea with Costa Rica. Table 1 shows that Costa Rica has much higher citizen life satisfaction, more positive

TABLE 1: South Korea versus Costa Rica, Life Conditions

	South Korea	Costa Rica
Household income (US$ per household)	$45,000	$12,800
Life satisfaction (on a scale of 1 to 10)	5.65	7.25
Positive feelings (% who feel positive)	67%	88%
Suicide rate (per 100,000)	24.1 (ranked 10th highest)	7.3 (ranked 124th)

SOURCES: Gallup World Poll, WHO (suicide rates).

feelings toward life and significantly lower suicide rates, despite having household incomes only 28% of that of South Korean households.

Who Are the Happiest Canadians of All?

In a 2010 study, *Does Money Matter: Determining the Happiness of Canadians*, researchers at the Ottawa-based Centre for Study of Living Standards found that the happiest Canadians have a strong sense of belonging to local communities. The sense of belonging was highest in smaller communities, rural areas and in Atlantic Canada. Quebec had the lowest sense of belonging, while Newfoundland had the highest.

Next in order of importance to the happiest communities was the level of perceived mental health, followed by physical activity levels, stress levels and being married. Communities with more new immigrants and with higher levels of unemployment rated more poorly in happiness. Unemployment is a particularly important driver of unhappiness. This study shows that, since there is sufficient evidence that mental health status, sense of belonging, physical health and stress levels are more significant determinants of happiness than household income, policy makers can focus more on these areas to improve the overall well-being in Canada.

The least important factor contributing to self-rated happiness was household income. The researchers concluded that more money does not translate into happier households. This is consistent with other studies by British economist Richard Easterlin, who found that both within and among nations, happiness varies directly with income but, over time, does not increase when a country's income increases.

Who are the happiest Canadians? In 2013, Statistics Canada showed that Prince Edward Island ranked first and Saskatchewan second, while my home province of Alberta ranked seventh in self-rated life satisfaction. In terms of cities, statistics for 2009–13 show that Sagenuenay (Quebec), Trois-Rivières (Quebec) and St. John's (Newfoundland) were the three happiest cities in Canada (Table 2). Vancouver and Toronto ranked last overall.

How efficient are Canadians in optimizing happiness for every dollar of household income? A simple ratio of life-satisfaction ratings for every $10,000 of household income shows that the top three Canadian cities optimizing happiness are Trois-Rivières (Quebec), Abbotsford (British Columbia) and Sherbrooke (Quebec). Calgary and Ottawa ranked last overall, despite having the highest median household incomes in Canada: $101,260 and $101,070 respectively.

Happiness as the Ultimate Objective of Economic Development

What if happiness and well-being were the ultimate goals of economic development policies in Alberta, Canada and all nations? What if Canada's prime minister or Alberta's premier built their political mandates on creating a flourishing economy of well-being modeled after Bhutan's Gross National Happiness? What if US and Canadian city councils were to adopt economic development objectives that are linked directly to improving well-being conditions, as the city of Victoria, British Columbia, has done recently?[18] The desired well-being outcomes for Victoria include increasing connections, belonging, trust and community cohesion. These social assets could be measured and reported on the city's balance sheet.

What if all political parties in Canada, the United States, Europe and Asia were to replace the current paradigm of economic

TABLE 2: Life Satisfaction of Canadian Cities, Ranked, Average: 2009–2013; scale: 1–10

Rank	City	Average Life Satisfaction (1–10)	Total Household income
	Canada (Average)	7.97	$76,550
1	Saguenay	8.25	$75,360
2	Trois-Rivières	8.18	$68,430
3	St. John's	8.17	$91,100
4	Greater Sudbury	8.17	$86,080
5	Quebec City	8.14	$84,160
6	Saint John	8.13	$73,600
7	Sherbrooke	8.11	$70,710
8	Thunder Bay	8.10	$82,690
9	Moncton	8.05	$73,550
10	Ottawa-Gatineau	8.05	$101,070
11	Saskatoon	8.02	$90,840
12	Kelowna	7.99	$76,870
13	Montreal	7.98	$73,250
14	Halifax	7.97	$82,510
15	Oshawa	7.96	$87,400
16	Calgary	7.96	$101,260
17	London	7.95	$75,980
18	Regina	7.94	$93,670
19	Kingston	7.94	$82,950
20	St. Catherines-Niagara	7.91	$69,500
21	Brantford	7.90	$71,630
22	Hamilton	7.90	$82,290
23	Winnipeg	7.89	$77,770
24	Abbotsford-Mission	7.89	$68,310
25	Kitchener-Waterloo	7.89	$82,160
26	Peterborough	7.89	$73,280
27	Victoria	7.89	$84,500
28	Barrie	7.88	$80,780
29	Edmonton	7.87	$98,480
30	Guelph	7.86	$88,700
31	Windsor	7.85	$73,440
32	Toronto	7.82	$72,830
33	Vancouver	7.81	$73,390

SOURCE: Statistics Canada. 2013. General Social Survey, 2009 to 2013, and Canadian Community Health Survey, 2009 to 2012. Annual Income for Census Families. Table 111-0009.

growth with a more compelling vision of improving the well-being bottom line? A more enlightened form of capitalism and governance based on optimizing the well-being returns on investment of a nation's five strategic assets is possible. It's a matter of volition. Why are these ideas for building common-sense economies of well-being not the central theme of discussions at the World Economic Forum or the G7/G20 gatherings? Why are these ideas not filling the pages of *The Economist*?

From Financial Capitalism to Well-being

What if the current dominant free-market financial capitalism were replaced with a new genuine wealth and well-being capitalism? If financial capitalism and economic development are characterized by the primacy of profit maximization and GDP growth, well-being capitalism would be characterized by economic development that increases the well-being of every citizen. Well-being returns, or impacts from investments in the human, social, natural and built or manufactured assets of a community, can be measured and thus incorporated into the annual budgets of all governments and corporations.

If financial capitalism is characterized by the lending of money at interest and the making of profits as part of the roundabout process by which it grows and hedges against inevitable risks, well-being capitalism would be characterized by creating money, without interest charges, in sufficient supply backed by the well-being benefits and utility of the assets of a community or nation. Ensuring the resilience of the human, social, natural and built assets of society would become the ultimate goal of governments.

Drowning in Debt

It has been eight years since the near death of Wall Street with the collapse of the financial markets in 2008. Not much has changed since then. The fundamental flaw of financial capitalism is in the very nature of money and how it is created. Nearly 98% of all money in our economies is debt-money, created primarily by private banks when they issue loans. While fractional reserve banking and money creation has been one of the greatest benefits of financial capitalism, fueling unprecedented economic and material prosperity, it comes at an enormous and hidden cost to all of society, including the environment.

The last available US Federal Reserve statistics, for the second quarter of 2017, show total debt outstanding in the United States of $68.0 trillion (household, business, government and foreign debt) or an estimated $530,064 per US household.[19] By its very definition, $68 trillion in total debt outstanding is the actual money supply of the United States, with only $1.5 trillion in paper currency in circulation in the US and globally. Therefore, paper money makes up only 2.18% of total money supply of the US. The US debts are broken down by sector as follows:

TABLE 3: US Debt Outstanding by Sector, 2017 (3rd Quarter)

Sector	Debt Outstanding (US$ billions)
Households (mortgages)	$10,009.9
Households (consumer credit)	$3,781.7
Business	$14,061.8
Federal Government	$16,463.2
State and Local Government	$3,042.7
Domestic Financial Sector	$15,888.6
Foreign debt	$3,493.8
Total Debts of the United States	$68,017.6

SOURCE: US Federal Reserve; data can be accessed December 8, 2017 federalreserve.gov/releases/z1/current /html/d3.htm Table D3. Debt Outstanding by Sector.

While the US Federal Reserve statistics estimate the US national (federal) debt at $16.5 trillion, US federal budget estimates projected it would reach over $20 trillion in 2017 or over 106% of US GDP.[20] In addition to financial debts, unfunded liabilities include social security liability (over $15.9 trillion) and Medicare liability (over $27.7 trillion).

The problem with debts is that they never get repaid. Instead they compound exponentially. The total US debt has been doubling roughly every six to ten years since World War II. In 1981, average ten-year Treasury yields averaged 13.92%, and total

US debt stood at $5.2 trillion. Within a little over six years US total debt had doubled, to over $11.5 trillion in 1988. It then took ten years to double again, reaching $23 trillion in 1998. Before the financial collapse in 2008, the total US debt was growing at an average rate of 8.9% per annum. Total debt outstanding actually fell by 0.3% in 2009 following the 2008 financial crisis, for the first time since 1947. Yet since 2010, debt money has resumed, with a 4.0% increase in total debts in 2016. While the US is fortunate to have record low interest rates, the fact that the total mountain of debt continues to grow means the cost of interest to American households and governments will continue to grow even larger, consuming an even larger portion of government and household budgets. Again, most are oblivious to this hidden cost of interest. Moreover, as debts continue to grow, there is continuous pressure for more economic (GDP) growth, which is necessary to service the interest costs of exponential debt growth. Debt is like a terminal cancer cell mass in the body of the economy. Unfortunately, there are currently no solutions or cures for the debt-money cancer that threatens virtually every economy on earth, from the wealthiest economies like the US and Canada all the way down to the poorest.

Debt and economic growth are directly related. When I run statistical correlation analysis between US GDP growth per capita and US total debts per capita, an extremely high (0.988) statistical correlation is found. The economy has to keep growing simply to service the exponentially growing mountain of outstanding debt, because of the increasing burden of interest costs associated with an ever-increasing mountain of unpaid debt. Moreover, every resource of the federal government is being utilized to spur more economic growth through loan guarantees, subsidized mortgage rates, low down payments, easy terms, tax credits, secondary markets, deposit insurances, etc. The reason for this policy is that the only way to make the consequences of the interest system bearable for the large majority of the population is to create a level of economic growth that follows the exponential growth rate of money—a vicious circle with an accelerating, spiraling effect.

According to US Federal Reserve statistics, the country's total outstanding debt per capita rose a staggering 5,000% between 1960 and 2016 (in 2016 dollars), compared with GDP per capita, which rose 1,876% (see Figure 9 in the following section). These debts came from both the private and public sector, the largest share coming from the private sector. Total outstanding debt has thus been rising faster than GDP and much faster than household income or wages, which have been virtually stagnant over the past thirty years.[21]

Using publicly available consumer/household debt statistics, business debt figures and public debt servicing costs, I have estimated a very conservative average total debt servicing cost of over $3.357 trillion in 2016, based on a very conservative 5.08% interest charge on the total $66 trillion in US debt: household/consumer debt (mortgages, students loans, credit cards), business debt (including business loans, farm credit), government debt (for municipal, state and federal government) and foreign debt (owed to foreigners or other nations).[22] It is very likely that the average interest rate on total US debt is higher than 5%. Yet even at these conservative levels, the total interest charges alone would equate to at least 18% of US GDP in 2016 (estimated at $18.560 trillion).[23] Compound interest in the economy acts like an invisible wrecking ball undermining the overall well-being aspirations of nations.

The Inconvenient Truth: How the Hidden Costs of Debt Are Killing American Happiness

Figure 9 shows the trend in average per capita US debt from 1960 to 2016 compared with US GDP per capita and the median household income of American households (1967–2015); all data are reported in 2016 dollars. The graph shows the growing burden of debt on American lives. In 1967, total US debt per household was roughly $21,708, or 357% of median household income of $6,087; in 2017 total outstanding US debt in the economy was projected to reach over $530,000, or 907% of median household income of an estimated $58,455 per annum. The same is true of total debt to GDP; in 2016 the US total debt to GDP ratio was 364%, a little lower than the peak of 381% in 2010, after the US financial crisis. The increase in total debt to household income is staggering. The burden these debts impose on all Americans is even more remarkable.

Since the cost of interest charges can be found in the prices of all goods and services, including government programs, services and taxes, every American is paying interest costs for everything they purchase. For, example the American household with a median income of $56,516 in 2016 spent roughly $28,267 of their pre-tax income on interest charges in their cost of housing, food, transportation, education, health-care, recreation and government services (paid through taxes). In simple terms, this means that the average American household will spend half or fifty cents or every dollar of earned income on hidden interest costs. Or put another way, the typical American household will work half of their lives simply working to pay the interest charges on a rising mountain of bank-created debt money.

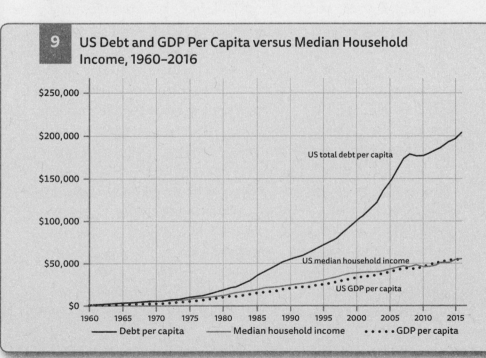

9 **US Debt and GDP Per Capita versus Median Household Income, 1960–2016**

SOURCE: US Federal Reserve Z.1 Financial Accounts of the United States (Table D3) Fourth Quarter, 2016; US Bureau of Economic Analysis (household income and US GDP historical statistics).

Moreover, lower-income households tend to pay disproportionately more in interest charges on the total debt of society than do upper-middle-class households. This is simply because higher-income-wealth households have more financial assets and investments that generate more interest income. There are indeed huge differences between who profits and who pays in this debt-money system. Breaking down household income into ten deciles or brackets shows that the first eight sections of the population pay more in interest charges on goods and services than they receive in interest income on investments, the ninth section receives slightly more than it pays, and the tenth receives about twice as much interest as it pays, i.e., the tenth receives the interest which the first eight sections have lost. This is why the rich get richer and the poor get poorer.

Remarkably, you will not find the cost of interest charges listed in the detailed household expenditure statistics collected by the US Bureau of Economic Analysis, along with shelter, food, transportation and taxes. Nor will you see these statistics reported by the US Federal Reserve bank, *The Economist*, *The New York Times* or *The Wall Street Journal*. This may be because most economists either do not consider debt money a problem or simply do not understand how debt money and interest relate to the economy and economic growth. Yet none of us escapes being touched or affected negatively by debt money bringing unaccountable levels of stress, anxiety and despair to our lives.

It is staggering to think that the greatest barriers to America's pursuit of happiness are never debated in the US Congress or state legislatures. Knowing there are legitimate alternatives to the current debt-money system to be found by re-examining the monetary policy history of the United States (including the ideas of Benjamin Franklin, Thomas Jefferson, Andrew Jackson, Abraham Lincoln and John F. Kennedy) compels all of us to explore new non-debt-asset-based money systems that exclude the burden of interest charges.

Until economists, national income accountants and political leaders acknowledge and account for the hidden cost to society of interest associated with debt, there is little hope for a sustainable economic future for all nations. We could envision a day when the current system of debt money will be deemed unconstitutional by hindering the pursuit of a good life, of life, liberty and the pursuit of happiness. In many ways, all of us have become unwitting debt-slaves in an economic system that is not of our design, which could be made more fair, just and transparent and could be oriented toward economic well-being goals.

However, a transition from the world's dominant debt-based money systems to one where money serves the well-being interests of all people will take either a catastrophic collapse in the current unsustainable debt-cancer system or an act of collective courage from world leaders. Removing the primary driver for economic growth and productivity, as shown by statistics, will ease the pressure on economies for more GDP growth and the pressure on households to make more money and accumulate financial wealth and material goods. Everyone would win in a world without debt money. Imagine a day when we need work only half the hours we currently do, with higher levels of happiness and well-being. This future is within our grasp within a single generation. A future with more joy in the form of more free time to spend with our children, parents, grandparents, friends and neighbors is possible.

The Path Ahead

It's time for a new, more common-sense economic, accounting and financial system that makes the old system of financial capitalism obsolete. We need to move away from narrow self-interest to an economy of sharing in the abundance of community assets, with a focus on reciprocal and thriving relationships where well-being benefits are optimized. Economies might be modeled after resilient natural ecosystems such as forests or watersheds.

I am under no illusion that building economies based on the real wealth and assets of the nation, backed by interest-free money and tied to the higher aspiration of well-being, will be easy. Many will claim that such a shift is impossible, utopian and unrealistic.

I believe otherwise. A shift to a total asset-based economic model is viable and within the scope of our existing economic, account-ing and financial systems. Moreover, a shift is possible simply because most people are finding that the current status quo has become unacceptable. At first, the steps toward an economy of well-being will be awkward and frustrating. I wrote this book be-cause I believe there are many people who yearn for a better and more hopeful future. From my experience I have seen that build-ing functional well-being economies is possible at any scale and in any sector. Nevertheless, the journey will require virtuous ac-tion, courage, patience, trial and error and wisdom. It will require a commitment to genuine engagement and active listening with our friends, neighbors, children, elders and politicians, rooted in the belief that all the solutions to our questions and challenges lie within the collective wisdom of the circle. Most importantly it will draw on our greatest strength and virtue: charity and love.

Notes

1. Thomas Aquinas said "To take interest for money lent is unjust in it-self, because this is to sell what does not exist, and this evidently leads to inequality, which is contrary to justice. Now, money was invented chiefly for the purpose of exchange. Hence, it is by its very nature unlawful to take payment for the use of money lent, which payment. (Thomas Aquinas (1269–71). *Summa Theologica*, translated by Fathers of the Dominican Province, pp. 330–340, R. T. Wasburne, Ltd. London, 1918.
2. Pope Francis (Jan 2014), addressing the National Council of Anti-Usury Foundations.
3. Eric Gallager. Aristotle's Definition of Eudaimonia. 11.24.2010. His-tory of Western Political Thought. Accessed at academia.edu/514238 /Aristotles_Definition_of_Eudaimonia December 18, 2016.
4. Ibid.
5. loc.gov/exhibits/treasures/trt001.html accessed December 18, 2016.
6. A steady-state economy is based on the principles of physics, in which an economy is founded on a constant stock of physical wealth (capital) that is maintained over time relative to a constant human population, such that in essence the economy does not grow. In fact, Adam Smith was the first to theorize that any national economy in the world would sooner or later settle into a final steady-state condition.

7. wellbeing.smgov.net/ accessed December 8, 2017.
8. gallup.com/poll/106756/galluphealthways-wellbeing-index.aspx accessed April 20, 2017.
9. gallup.com/opinion/gallup/206468/happiest-unhappiest-countries-world.aspx?g_source=CATEGORY_WELLBEING&g_medium=topic &g_campaign=tiles accessed April 20, 2017.
10. Harris Poll results are for 2008–2016. Other US happiness polls are from various previous surveys dating back to 1946.
11. theharrispoll.com/health-and-life/American-Happiness-at-All-Time -Low.html Harris Poll has been measuring Americans' happiness since 2008 using an index that is calculated by taking an average of those who *strongly agree* with certain positive statements and *strongly disagree* with certain negative statements that are asked along an agree/ disagree scale.
12. time.com/4389726/harris-poll-happiness-index-2016/.
13. Based on analysis conducted by Mark Anielski using US Federal Reserve US debt statistics, GDP and other economic statistics for the period 1950 to 2017.
14. According to the 2017 US federal budget, health care spending was estimated to be $1,254.8 billion and defense budget was $808.3 billion. Estimated total, or gross, interest payments on the US federal debt ($21,325.5 billion) was estimated at $928.8 billion.
15. Based on US Households by Total Money Income, Race, and Hispanic Origin of Householder: 1967 to 2015, US Census Bureau, Current Population Survey, 1967 through 2016 Annual Social and Economic Supplements.
16. ons.gov.uk/peoplepopulationandcommunity/wellbeing/bulletins /measuringnationalwellbeing/2015to2016 accessed May 31, 2017.
17. Ed Diener speaking in Singapore in 2016 youtu.be/jCrOpCGdEvI.
18. The City of Victoria, BC, led by Mayor Lisa Helps, has developed a new economic development strategy, Making Victoria: Unleashing Potential, which states, "The ultimate purpose of economic development is to increase the genuine well-being of citizens. Well-being is defined as a state of complete physical, mental and social well-being and not merely the absence of disease or infirmity (World Health Organization)." victoria.ca/EN/main/business/economic-development.html, accessed May 29, 2017.
19. Official total debt statistics for the US are reported quarterly by the US Federal Reserve; data can be accessed at federalreserve.gov/releases /z1/Current/ Table D3. At the end of the 3rd quarter 2017 total outstanding US debt was $68,017 billion.
20. As of March 2017, the US debt is about $19.9 trillion and is constantly changing; it amounts to:

$61,365 for every person living in the US
$158,326 for every household in the US
106% of the US gross domestic product
560% of annual federal revenues

Much of the debt is bought and held by individuals, institutional investment companies and foreign governments. The debt is managed by the US Treasury. usnews.com/news/economy/articles/2017-04-13/what-are-the-national-debt-debt-ceiling-and-budget-deficit, accessed May 31, 2017.

21. Analysis is based on US Federal Reserve statistics of historical total debt in the US and US GDP statistics from the US Bureau of Economic Analysis.

22. These figures vary from an estimated average 6.46% interest charges on household debt (mortgages, consumer credit, credit card debt, student loans, etc.), to 4.15% average interest charge on all federal, state and local government debt and 5.00% average interest charges on business, domestic financial sector and foreign debts. Experts with greater knowledge of the actual interest rate charges on all forms of debt will undoubtedly see that my interest rate cost estimates are highly conservative.

23. See bea.gov/newsreleases/national/gdp/gdpnewsrelease.htm, accessed May 31, 2017.

CHAPTER 2

A Roadmap to Well-Being

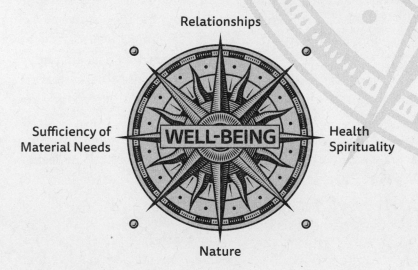

IT WOULD BE NICE to think that the path to an economy of well-being will be as simple as a well-being compass and a map following Dorothy along the yellow brick road to visit the Wizard of Oz for guidance. But Dorothy and her colleagues learned that the solutions they were looking for (a brain, a heart, courage, a return to Kansas) were to be found within themselves. The practical tools and processes for designing and building an economy of well-being will likewise be found within our communities and driven by our convictions that a new paradigm is possible.

Can Well-Being be Measured?

One of the questions I am often asked is, Can well-being and happiness actually be measured? Based on the recently released *World Happiness Report*, economics, psychologists, social scientists and others are demonstrating that it is possible. Moreover, when something can be measured, it becomes a science and thus achieves some sense of legitimacy.

New surveys such as the Gallup World Poll (GWP), the World Values Survey (WVS) and others have been designed specifically to measure subjective well-being, asking people to rate their life satisfaction (today), their current perceptions of happiness, their sense of their happiness yesterday (remembered well-being: "Overall, how happy were you yesterday?") and the positive affects (e.g., enjoyment, happiness, laughter) and negative affects (e.g., worry, sadness, anger, depression) these factors have on happiness. When life satisfaction, happiness and these other factors are measured, they tell a very similar story about the likely sources of a good life.

A common set of objective determinants of subjective well-being are emerging, suggesting we can combine both subjective happiness surveys with regular monitoring of the conditions of well-being that are known to contribute to higher self-rated life satisfaction and happiness. Happier nations (which include Denmark, Finland and Canada) tend to have higher average incomes, healthy life expectancy and a stronger sense of personal freedom; their citizens are less likely to perceive widespread corruption in business and government and are more likely to have someone they can call on in times of trouble.

Research has revealed strong correlations between life circumstances (conditions of well-being) and subjective well-being, or happiness, and shown that many subjective measures of well-being are highly correlated with objective measures, such as facial expressions, brain-wave patterns and cortisol levels in individuals, as well as community and national suicide patterns. Measures of subjective well-being can be used to predict subsequent events and behaviors that are important to local governance. For example, many happiness measures are predictive of sickness, so that collecting them on a regular basis could be part of health maintenance and the delivery of health services. Another example is that people with disabilities tend to have lower subjective well-being ratings, which are connected to an individual's ability to maintain strong social connections.

According to some researchers, happiness follows a U shape, or smiley face, pattern over the course of a human lifespan (see Figure 10). We are happiest at a young age (before puberty) and again in old age (65 years+). Happiness, or life satisfaction, declines sometime after 11 to 12 years of age and then nosedives between 40 and 50. "Human happiness hits the lowest point around the ages of 40 to 42," writes Melbourne University researcher Dr. Terence Cheng, who led a longitudinal study into the U-bend phenomenon.[1] But don't worry, even as you reach the bottom of your happiness curve in your forties, you have another 30 years or more to recalibrate, count your blessings and pursue a life of purpose and work that brings genuine meaning and joy.

Efforts to measure and promote happiness can be set within a broader accounting framework of measuring and reporting well-being, as proposed by Bhutan's prime minister Jigme Y. Thinley at the 2012 High-Level Meeting on Wellbeing and Happiness at the United Nations. At that meeting the French president, Nicolas

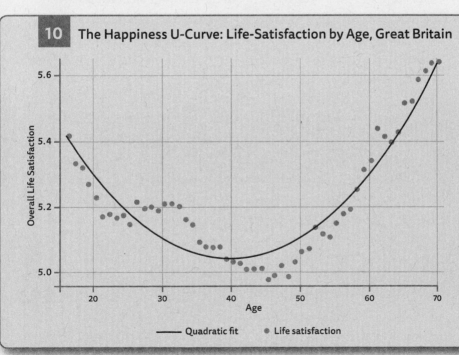

10   The Happiness U-Curve: Life-Satisfaction by Age, Great Britain

— Quadratic fit   ● Life satisfaction

NOTE: Each dot measures the mean life-satisfaction of individuals of that particular age.
SOURCE: Terence C. Cheng, Nattavudh Powdthavee, Andrew J. Oswald. 2014. Longitudinal Evidence for a Midlife Nadir in Human Well-Being: Results from Four Data Sets. IZA Discussion Paper. No. 7942, February 2014.

Sarkozy, noted that the global financial and European debt crises compelled nations to imagine other economic models and new measures of progress to GDP, such as Bhutan was advocating. The British prime minister, David Cameron, brought well-being into the UK's core measures of progress, declaring:

> Improving our society's sense of well-being is the central political challenge of our times. It's time we admitted that there's more to life than money, and it's time we focused not just on GDP, but on GWB—general well-being.... Well-being can't be measured by money or traded in markets. It's about the beauty of our surroundings, the quality of our culture, and above all the strength of our relationships."[2]

While interest in this new economic paradigm of well-being may seem to have waned in the past two years, I would suggest that the urgency of adopting a new well-being economic model and accounting system is even greater today. Significant advances in the science of well-being and the measurement of well-being conditions, as well as new well-being indices and governance systems that link economic development to well-being, particularly at the municipal level, have been emerging since the 2012 meeting in New York. What is required is a commitment of politicians across all political spectrums to adopt a system of national and regional well-being accounting and reporting similar to national income accounting and GDP reporting adopted after World War II.

A well-being accounting system would require collecting a broader set of information on the five capitals of a community's assets (human, social, natural, built and financial capital assets) that are relevant to the understanding and improvement of well-being in the community. In this system, subjective well-being data and scores can be seen as directly democratic measures of the quality of individual and community life within a geographic area (e.g., community, neighborhoods). Objective well-being data and indices can also be used to evaluate well-being conditions that contribute most to subjective well-being, also within and across geographic areas and in the context of ecosystem boundaries.

This commitment to measuring and reporting both subjective and objective well-being would improve the capacity of decision-makers in a community to build and enhance overall well-being in support of the good life for all. More comprehensive assessments of "returns to well-being" that go beyond conventional benefit/ cost analysis are possible. In the same way we can demonstrate the real value that stems from taxes and programs that invest in building the genuine wealth (improved well-being) of communities. It would thus be possible to design, build and assess the relative importance of various policies and programs in terms of improving well-being conditions and reducing negative conditions or liabilities to happiness that might arise in communities.

The Science of Well-Being:
What We Measure Affects What We Do

Over the past ten years a growing number of positive psychologists and progressive economists have begun to articulate the science of well-being. Studies show that the key contributors to a happy life are the quality of one's upbringing and genetics (50%) and the strength and quality of one's relationships with family, friends and work colleagues (40%); income and education are a distant third (only 10%). New research suggests that the experience of one's childhood years, more than genetics, may be the most important contribution to one's sense of well-being throughout life.

According to economists John Helliwell (University of British Columbia), Jeffrey Sachs (London School of Economics) and Richard Layard (Columbia University)—authors of the first UN *World Happiness Report*, published in 2012—a new generation of studies by psychologists, economists, pollsters, sociologists and others has shown that happiness, though indeed a subjective experience, can be objectively measured, assessed, correlated with observable brain functions and related to the characteristics of an individual and their society. Asking people whether they are happy or satisfied with their lives offers important information about society. It can signal underlying crises or hidden strengths. It can suggest the need for change.

According to the *World Happiness Report*, the difference in the level of happiness nations experience depends on six key variables:
1. real gross domestic product (GDP) per capita,
2. healthy life expectancy,
3. having someone to count on,
4. perceived freedom to make life choices,
5. generosity and,
6. freedom from corruption.[3]

Positive psychologist Martin Seligman has argued that the science of well-being and happiness, also known as positive psychology, has advanced to the point that we can now measure certain forms of happiness. Seligman has established a model for measuring well-being, PERMA, which looks at five attributes of well-being (2011):[4]
1. **P**ositive emotions refer to hedonic feelings of happiness (e.g., feeling joyful, content and cheerful).
2. **E**ngagement refers to psychological connection to activities or organizations (e.g., feeling absorbed, interested and engaged in life).
3. **R**elationships include feeling socially integrated, cared about and supported by others, and satisfied with one's social connections.
4. **M**eaning refers to believing that one's life is valuable and feeling connected to something greater than oneself.
5. **A**ccomplishment involves making progress toward goals, feeling capable of doing daily activities and having a sense of achievement.

Seligman believes that these five pillars—all important areas of life that people pursue for their own sake—contribute to their overall state of well-being. The emergence of such a science of well-being suggests that it can become a fundamental feature of economics, accounting and governance.

Maslow's Hierarchy of Needs and an Indigenous Model of Well-Being

Many of us are familiar with Abraham Maslow's hierarchy-of-needs model for defining levels of needs and wants, which run from food and shelter to higher aspirations including spiritual well-being and enlightenment. Maslow's model could be used as the basis of a well-being assessment and reporting system.

Where did Maslow get his ideas for a hierarchy of needs? According to a Canadian Indigenous scholar, University of Alberta PhD candidate Karen Pheasant, Abraham Maslow based his model on his study of the Blackfoot Indigenous people of southern Alberta and their medicine wheel model, which says that all people are made up of four integrated aspects: mental, physical, emotional and spiritual.[5] All four aspects are considered to be equal and balanced in harmony with each other in a circle. This suggests that for Indigenous peoples, life was seen not as a

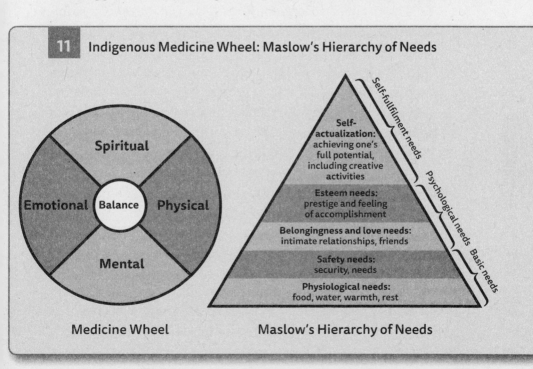

11 Indigenous Medicine Wheel: Maslow's Hierarchy of Needs

Medicine Wheel

Maslow's Hierarchy of Needs

pyramid to ascend but rather a hoop or circle, driven by free will or volition through time. In this view, a circle or flower seems to be the most appropriate image of human flourishing. In the center of the circle are balance, harmony and, ultimately, flourishing well-being.

The Util: Measuring Real Utility

John Stuart Mill (1806–73) provided us with the theory of utilitarianism (1863), which he based on the principle that "actions are right in proportion as they tend to promote happiness, wrong as they tend to produce the reverse of happiness." Mill defined happiness as pleasure and the absence of pain. He argued that pleasure can differ in quality and quantity, and that pleasures that are rooted in one's higher faculties should be weighted more heavily than baser pleasures. Furthermore, Mill argued that people's achievement of goals and ends, such as virtuous living, should be counted as part of their happiness.[6]

Mill was influenced by Jeremy Bentham (1748–1832), whose formulation of utilitarianism was known as the "greatest-happiness principle." It holds that one must always act to produce the greatest aggregate happiness among all sentient beings, within reason. Bentham's fundamental axiom was the principle that "it is the greatest happiness of the greatest number that is the measure of right and wrong."[7] He treated all forms of happiness as equal, whereas Mill argued that intellectual and moral pleasures (higher pleasures) are superior to more physical forms of pleasure (lower pleasures). Mill distinguishes between happiness and contentment, claiming that the former is of higher value than the latter.[8]

Utility has been the basis of my economic training since undergraduate economics. Economic utility is defined as a measure of preferences over some set of goods (including services: something that satisfies human wants); it represents satisfaction experienced by the consumers of those goods. Economists typically measure utility in terms of the relationship between the demand (measured in terms of prices and thus money units) and supply (quantity of goods or services). Since economists cannot directly measure benefit, satisfaction or happiness from a good or service, they have devised ways of representing and measuring utility in terms of measurable economic choices. The measures typically take the form of units of money or currency, which are not necessarily connected to genuine well-being as they are not derived from assets. When the nature of money and its creation is properly understood—created *ex nihilo* (out of nothing) and connected to no assets—we are left to question whether there are more meaningful measures of utility.

What does a util, or unit of utility, actually measure beyond some monetary measure of consumer preference? Might Mills agree that a util could be defined as a measure of well-being or well-being impact? If so, this would change the very nature of the economist utility-maximization model. The concept of utility to economists underpins rational choice theory and game theory.

When the theories of utilitarianism combine with the emerging science of well-being, then a solid foundation for an architecture of an economy of well-being emerges. This would be further advanced by building on the original accounting principles of the 15th-century Italian mathematician Luca Pacioli and his collaborator Leonardo da Vinci.

Without Virtue, Happiness Cannot Be

Etymologically, the word *virtue* comes from the 13th-century word *vertu*, which means "moral life and conduct; a particular moral excellence." Virtues, by definition, refer to a set of core values or desired actions for a good life that we all hold in common. By definition, a virtue is a quality considered morally good or desirable in a person. For example, patience is a virtue. I believe that one of the key reasons for the problems of the world is that we have forgotten the virtues. No longer do we examine our actions in the mirror of virtues, as Benjamin Franklin once did. Our economic models are not tied to virtues but to economic growth, profit maximization and the servicing of financial debts.

Benjamin Franklin, one of the founding fathers of the United States, established his own set of personal and social virtues, which he used to examine his own conscience and behavior each night before going to sleep. Here are Franklin's seven personal virtues:[9]

+ **Temperance:** Eat not to dullness; drink not to elevation.
+ **Resolution:** Resolve to perform what you ought; perform without fail what you resolve.
+ **Frugality:** Make no expense but to do good to others or yourself; i.e., waste nothing.
+ **Moderation:** Avoid extremes; forbear resenting injuries so much as you think they deserve.
+ **Industry:** Lose no time; be always employed in something useful; cut off all unnecessary actions.
+ **Cleanliness:** Tolerate no uncleanliness in body, clothes, or habitation.
+ **Tranquility:** Be not disturbed at trifles, or at accidents.

Franklin also examined his own conscience through a series of social virtues that included

+ **Silence:** Speak not but what may benefit others or yourself; avoid trifling conversation.
+ **Sincerity:** Use no hurtful deceit; think innocently and justly, and, if you speak, speak accordingly.
+ **Justice:** Wrong none by doing injuries, or omitting the benefits that are your duty.
+ **Chastity:** Rarely use venery but for health or offspring, never to dullness, weakness, or the injury of your own or another's peace or reputation.
+ **Order:** Let all your things have their places; let each part of your business have its time.
+ **Humility:** Imitate Jesus and Socrates.

Imagine if today's world government and business leaders adopted Franklin's practice of examining their actions in the mirror of a set of societal virtues. I suggest that an economy of well-being be governed based on a set of common virtues that constitute

12   World Virtues and Well-Being Thematic Framework

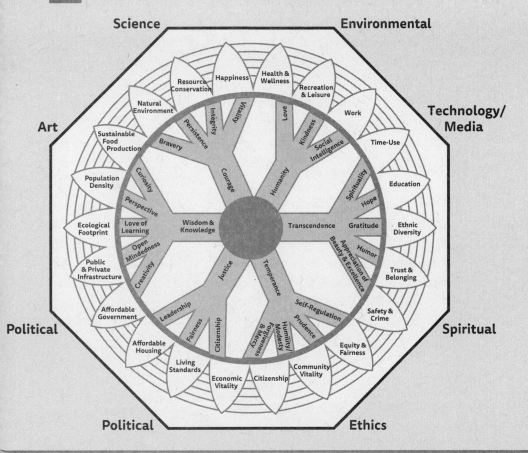

SOURCE: Renee Bunnell-Schwartz. 2010. "Mapping Sustainable Abundance: Towards a Broad Integration of Psychological and Economic Well-Being." Unpublished white paper written for Fielding Graduate University toward a PhD dissertation.

behavioral qualities of a good life founded on the adage of doing well by doing good.

The virtues-well-being framework (Figure 12) was developed by Dr. Renee Bunnell-Schwartz, a New York-based positive psychologist. She attempted to integrate psychological and economic well-being attributes using a synthesis of common virtues from across world religions and 23 well-being themes (taken from my 2006 well-being assessment of the City of Leduc, Alberta).

Bunnell-Schwartz developed her model to help future clients self-assess their lives and actions through a set of common virtues. She reasoned as long as someone was aware of the congruence of their actions and known virtues, it was possible for them to live a life of sustainable abundance. The mandala-like image of sustainable abundance is similar to the flower or spider graphics of well-being you will find further on in my book. This compass for living is similar to the Indigenous medicine wheel or hoop of life, with its four directions or aspects of a human being: mental, spiritual, emotional and physical well-being.

The Five Capital Assets of Well-Being

What is an asset? The word has its etymological roots in the 1530s, when it was defined as "sufficient estate," from Anglo-French *assetz*, from Old French *assez*: "sufficiency, satisfaction; compensation." According to the modern dictionary definition, an asset is

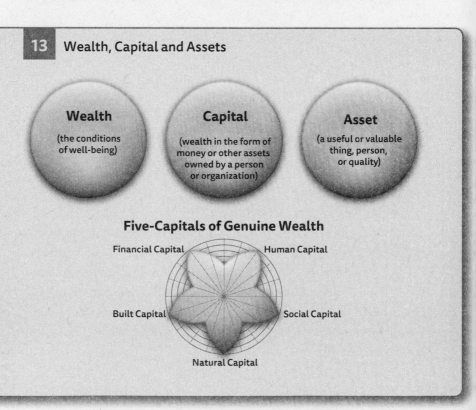

13   Wealth, Capital and Assets

Wealth
(the conditions of well-being)

Capital
(wealth in the form of money or other assets owned by a person or organization)

Asset
(a useful or valuable thing, person, or quality)

Five-Capitals of Genuine Wealth

Financial Capital   Human Capital

Built Capital   Social Capital

Natural Capital

"anything tangible or intangible that can be owned or controlled to produce value and that is held to have positive economic value" to its owners. To an economist or accountant, assets represent value of ownership that can be converted into cash (which is also considered an asset).

Economic historian and author Robert McGarvey points out that at the very core of an economy lie its asset foundations, the DNA of capitalism. McGarvey notes,

> Assets are institutional "vessels" that capture and store human energy and other forms of economically important value. The institutional support assets enjoy from managers, accountants, bankers and others create their unique "buoyancy," allowing the value in assets to rise (or fall) in a leveraged fashion with the ebb and flow of economic currents. Assets buttress the economy because the stored value in assets can be owned by an individual (or corporation) and leveraged to create liquidity for all kinds of productive purposes. Assets play a critical role in capitalism, their unique characteristics determining the structure and form of all subsequent economic organization.[10]

I propose that the definition of an asset be broadened to include anything tangible or intangible that contributes to the well-being of an individual, family, organization, community, nation or natural ecosystem. Broadening the definition would allow accountants and economists to expand the scope of measurement and reporting to including intangible assets such as trust, goodwill, relationships and other forms of social capital in addition to natural capital assets (forests, wetlands, carbon) and ecological goods and services. These well-being assets would then become the basis of sustainable livelihoods (as per the Brundtland Commission model of 1989) for individuals, communities and accounting systems that align with the new United Nations Sustainable Development Goals (2016).[11]

It is possible to add this broader suite of intangible assets to the balance sheet of communities and companies. This kind of management accounting of non-traditional assets would become of strategic importance to any organization, community or government that wishes to demonstrate the value these assets contribute to the well-being of society.

This accounting approach can be rationalized by using the original English definition of wealth,[12] namely the "conditions of well-being," and recognizing that one definition of capital is "any form of wealth employed or capable of being employed in the production of more wealth."[13] Expanding the suite of assets to be measured will require new inventory, accounting and asset valuation and verification protocols. Many new assets will need to be qualified through qualitative assessment tools, including well-being rating systems and proxies.

As proposed in *The Economics of Happiness: Building Genuine Wealth* (2007), an integrated five-capital asset accounting and reporting system would facilitate this new approach to accountancy. The five-capital asset model of human, social, natural, built and financial assets can be applied at any level of reporting, on the scale of the individual, the household, the community, the municipality, the organization or firm, the nation or even the ecosystem or watershed.

The five capitals under management in a well-being economy are shown in Figure 14 and can be further delineated as follows:
+ **Human capital:** workers' skills and abilities as regards their contribution to an economy:
    + Positive psychological capital; the value of an individual's level of optimism, hope, resilience, self-efficacy;
    + Intellectual capital; intangible assets, for example, knowledge, resource know-how and understanding of processes.
+ **Social capital:** the web and value of interpersonal connections, networks and relationships:
    + Political capital, the means by which a politician or political party may gain support or popularity;
    + Cultural capital, the advantage individuals can gain

14   Five Capitals of the Well-Being Economy

Financial Capital

Financial assets (money, cash, stocks, bonds, derivatives), liabilities (debt) and equity.

Human Capital

Individual skills, education, knowledge, capabilities, and health (mental, physical, emotional, and spiritual) of individuals that make up households, organizations and communities.

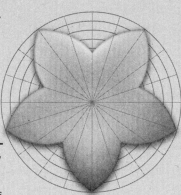

Built Capital

Infrastructure, buildings, roads, houses, factories, machinery, equipment, and manufactured goods and intellectual property (patents, copyright) that make up the material structure of society

Social Capital

The web of interpersonal connections, relationships and networks, including trust, institutional arrangements, rules, and norms that facilitate human interactions. Also, the set of values, history, traditions and behaviors that link a specific group or people together.

Natural Capital

The land and natural resources, including soils, forests, water, air, and other species and life forms, and the services which the Earth and its atmosphere provide, including ecological systems and life-support services.

from mastering the cultural tastes of a privileged group;

 + Symbolic capital, language and/or images that circulate as power. According to Pierre Bourdieu, symbolic capital is strongly correlated to social capital and comes into existence once it is perceived and recognized as legitimate.

+ **Natural capital:** the resources of an ecosystem that yield a flow of goods and services into the future.

+ **Built capital:** means of production other than natural capital; any non-human asset made by humans and then used in production.

+ **Financial capital:** any form of wealth capable of being employed in the production of more wealth.

Well-Being Accounts

Professor Ed Diener, a leading positive psychologist, has suggested establishing a set of national (and state-level) well-being accounts to help govern society.[14] Just as macro-economists construct national income accounts from which GDP is derived as a measure of economic progress, a set of five-capital asset accounts would provide a more robust accounting for the well-being of a municipality, state, province or nation.

Well-being accounts would include the current conditions of both objective and subjective well-being for each of the five asset classes, drawing from conventional statistics on the conditions of societal well-being along with subjective measures from surveys of citizens who provide self-rated scores to questions ranging from their life satisfaction and mental, spiritual and workplace well-being to relationships and trust of others and their perceptions of personal flourishing and mastery of skills.

A system of well-being accounts would help make governments accountable to their citizens with respect to what we all want: the highest possible conditions of well-being for ourselves, our families, our communities and the environment. Such measures of well-being would complement existing measures of economic progress such as GDP, not replace them entirely. In other words, they would provide the basis for demonstrating the value of taxes, programs and services and "measure what matters" to citizens.

Why would we want to monitor well-being? Because, as Diener notes, we have something to gain as a society when people are flourishing because of their state of well-being and contributing to the rest of the community and society in a net positive way. Increasing sustainable well-being would become the highest aspiration of government accountability.

I believe well-being as a desired future is easier to explain to citizens than narrower measures like GDP. It is also easier to demonstrate well-being value impacts relative to capital and operating budgets of all levels of government.

The Five-Assets Sustainable
Livelihood Model for Measuring Assets

The Sustainable Livelihood Asset Model, developed in the early 1990s as an outcome of the Brundtland Commission work on sustainable development, provides a good framework for assessing individual and community assets (see Figure 15). The model uses five asset classes (personal, human, social, physical, financial) and six sub-asset characteristics, recognizing that everyone has assets on which to build and support individuals and families so they in turn can acquire the assets needed for long-term well-being.

The Brundtland Commission defined sustainable livelihood as follows:

> A livelihood comprises the capabilities, assets (stores, resources, claims and access) and activities required for a means of living: a livelihood is sustainable which can cope

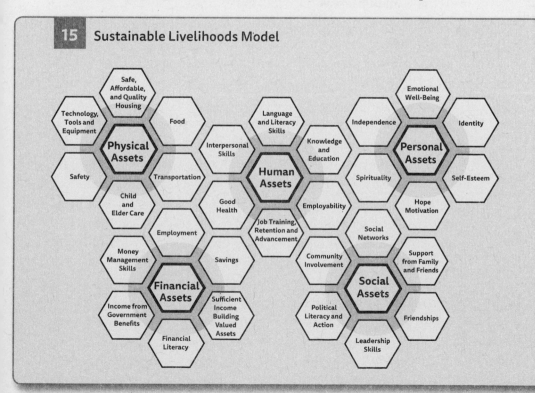

15 Sustainable Livelihoods Model

SOURCE: Department for International Development. (1999). Sustainable Livelihoods Guidance Sheet: Introduction. livelihoods.org/info/info_guidancesheets.html#1.

with and recover from stress and shocks, maintain or enhance its capabilities and assets, and provide sustainable livelihood opportunities for the next generation; and which contributes net benefits to other livelihoods at the local and global levels and in the short and long term.[15]

This definition is closely aligned with the City of Edmonton's working definition of poverty, which focused on an individual's lack of access to the resources needed to participate fully in society. In 2016, the city set an ambitious goal of eliminating poverty within a generation through the EndPovertyEdmonton initiative. As a measurement adviser to the initiative, I proposed the sustainable livelihoods framework as a way of tracking the success of lifting ten thousand Edmontonians out of poverty within five years, the target set by the city. I suggested that this model could be used to assess the individual and household assets of people living in financial poverty. Investing in strengthening these assets could then be the key to end poverty for these people.

To understand the pathway out of poverty to well-being, I believe we need to understand the key drivers that give rise to poverty. The relative socioeconomic conditions that currently result in conditions of poverty (measured currently in terms of low-income conditions) can be assessed, as can the relative impact of policy changes, interventions/innovations and other strategies/ actions to alleviate the conditions of living that result in poverty, i.e., the lack or inaccessibility of resources (deficits) that stop people from achieving a given standard of livelihood. While poverty tends to focus on the lack of life resources, an asset-based approach looks at what resources people currently have for a certain quality of life.

The sustainable livelihoods model provides a good visualization of how poverty-elimination initiatives can lift people out of poverty into a flourishing state of well-being. It involves taking an asset-building approach to solving some of society's greatest challenges. Asset-building actions may include providing low-cost, sustainable, affordable housing through models like Habitat for Humanity, which I discuss later. Other efforts might include a living-wage policy for cities that encourages all employers to appreciate what a living wage is and make sure that their employees receive such a wage.

Using a sustainable livelihoods model to measure the success of actions to eliminate poverty can be an effective means of demonstrating progress and the value of investments made to build up assets and therefore overall community well-being. Other key measures of happiness, including a stronger sense of belonging and inclusion in society, will also become key measures of success. The model recognizes that everyone needs certain assets if they are to achieve long-term well-being, and then it works to support individuals and families in acquiring or building these assets. It may focus on a more limited (e.g., specifically economic) or wider set of assets (e.g., personal, cultural, social, political).

The Well-Being Economy and UN Sustainable Development Goals

In an attempt to describe "the future we want" for the world in terms of sustainable development, the United Nations recently established 17 Sustainable Development Goals (SDGs), 169 targets

16   United Nations' Sustainable Development Goals

1 NO POVERTY
2 NO HUNGER
3 GOOD HEALTH
4 QUALITY EDUCATION
5 GENDER EQUALITY
6 CLEAN WATER AND SANITATION
7 RENEWABLE ENERGY
8 GOOD JOBS AND ECONOMIC GROWTH
9 INNOVATION AND INFRASTRUCTURE
10 REDUCED INEQUALITIES
11 SUSTAINABLE CITIES AND COMMUNITIES
12 RESPONSIBLE CONSUMPTION
13 CLIMATE ACTION
14 LIFE BELOW WATER
15 LIFE ON LAND
16 PEACE AND JUSTICE
17 PARTNERSHIPS FOR THE GOALS

THE GLOBAL GOALS
For Sustainable Development

SOURCE: United Nations. sustainabledevelopment.un.org/?menu=1300 accessed May 30, 2017.

and 304 indicators. Taken together, the SDGs could be viewed as a set of human rights that amount to an economy of well-being, though they are not specifically designed with that aspiration in mind. One of their shortcomings is that while the goals are aspirational and may lead to a more sustainable economy, they are not grounded in any theoretical model or science of well-being. Moreover, the proposed goals, actions and indicators are not organized within an asset accounting model.

For many nations, particularly developed nations like Canada, the US and European nations, the 17 SDGs are a checklist of goals they will have already achieved, with some exceptions such as pockets of poverty amongst certain cohorts of the population (e.g., First Nations in Canada).

Let us apply, for example, the number one goal of ending poverty to my own city of Edmonton, Canada. In my role in the End-PovertyEdmonton task force, I suggested that one way of ending poverty in wealthy countries like Canada is to commit to ensuring that people earn a living wage—a wage sufficient to meet life's needs. This would require a commitment by both public sector and businesses to ensure that all citizens can meet basic life needs and participate fully in society. This raises the question: on a global scale, what would it cost to eliminate poverty by guaranteeing every person a living wage?

In 2015, an estimated 935 million people (12.7% of the world's population) were living below the extreme poverty line of $1.90 per day, or $694 per year. About half of the world's people (over 3.2 billion) live on $2.50 per day, while four out of five (5.15 billion) live on $10 per day or less. The richest 1% (about 73 million) own half of the world's total wealth of $125 trillion.

According to *Forbes* magazine, there were an estimated 123,800 multimillionaires in 2015, of which 1,810 were billionaires. Their aggregate net worth was $6.48 trillion, or an average of $3.58 billion each. The combined wealth of the world's 1,810 billionaires was $6.48 trillion, 1.4 times more than the GDP of Japan (the world's third largest economy, with a GDP of US$4.7 trillion) or 35% of the GDP of the United States (the world's largest economy, with a GDP of US$18.6 trillion). Some economists, including Jeffrey Sachs, author of *The End of Poverty: Economic Possibilities for Our Time* (2005), have proposed providing a cash transfer of 50 cents a day or $200 per year to the estimated 650 million living in extreme poverty (on less than $1.90 per day or $694 per year).

Based on these figures, the total annual cost of eliminating poverty for the world's extremely poor would be a mere $130 billion: 0.11% of the world's total GDP [16] (US$119.4 trillion, estimated in purchase price parity or PPP),[17] or only 2.0% of the total net worth of the world's 1,810 billionaires.[18] This would constitute a bold step in achieving the first UN SDG goal of eliminating poverty.

However, this still does not help the billions of people who are not earning a living wage from their labor. I have estimated that about five billion people (more than two-thirds of the world's population) live below a living wage. This amount varies from one country to the next; in Africa, for instance, a living wage can range from US$3.58 to $14.39 per day; in Edmonton it is roughly $140.00 per day ($17.56 per hour).[19] If we assume a median living wage of US$9.00/day for Africa and apply this to the five billion people living below a living wage, then the estimated annual global cost of paying a living wage increment would be roughly $11.7 trillion per annum, or 9.8% of the world's annual GDP. This is slightly higher than China's GDP of $11.4 trillion. Adding $11.7 trillion in global disposable income would be like adding the spending power of another China, the world's second-largest economy.

Of course, eliminating poverty is not simply about improving the wages of the poor; poverty includes a lack of services and access to education, employment, and decision-making. SDG Goal #3 is to "ensure healthy lives and promote well-being for all at all ages." This is more of an issue in developing nations than it is in countries like Canada with high life expectancy, generally higher rates of health, access to clean drinking water and very low rates of pollution-related illnesses.

Some have criticized the SDGs for being contradictory, because in seeking high levels of global GDP growth, they will undermine their own ecological objectives. In my opinion, their weakness

from an economic perspective is the fact that they are not connected to an accounting architecture such as the five-asset capital
model I have proposed for nations and governments. That does
not preclude municipal, provincial or national governments
adopting the 17 SDGs within a five-capital asset accounting and
reporting model based on the science of well-being. Many of the
SDGs and the targets and progress indicators are similar to the objective and subjective well-being indicators I have used to evaluate community well-being in Canada.

Well-Being-Based Governments

At the municipal, provincial or state, or national level, well-being
can be made the central organizing principle and aspiration for
any society. At present, most economies are governed to achieve
high levels of economic progress as measured by a single performance measure, the GDP. Making well-being the central governing principle would provide governments of all levels with
the capacity to not only measure what matters to most citizens
(namely, the well-being of their families and communities) but
also be a means of demonstrating value for programs, services
and taxes.

New public sector accounting systems that measure well-being
conditions and progress will be necessary to supplement and even
replace the dominant money measures of progress such as the
GDP. New indices such as the Canadian Index of Wellbeing (CIW)
can allow governments at all levels to measure and monitor well-
being conditions relative to an economy's GDP. The CIW measures
eight domains of well-being: education, living standards, community vitality, democratic engagement, healthy populations, time
use, leisure and culture, and the environment. While it's an intu-
itively attractive alternative measure of progress, the CIW has yet
to be fully adopted at any level of Canadian government, national,
provincial or municipal.

The CIW analysis for 2106 shows that Canada's GDP per capita
grew by 38.0% between 1994 and 2014, while the CIW grew 9.9%.

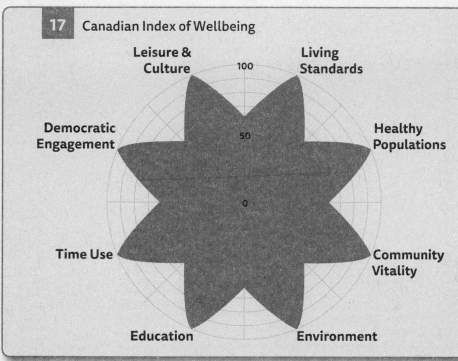

17 Canadian Index of Wellbeing

SOURCE: The Canadian Index of Wellbeing, uwaterloo.ca/canadian-index-wellbeing/. The stylized CIW image was created by Mark Anielski based on the CIW domains of well-being.

University of Waterloo researchers now maintain that the Canadian economy, despite faltering briefly after the 2008 recession, has since recovered, based on GDP. But the gap between the growth in per capita GDP and Canadians' well-being has been growing wider since the recession; in 2007, it was 22.0%, but by 2014 it had jumped to 28.1%. In terms of overall well-being conditions, Canadians are losing valuable leisure time, feeling an increasing time crunch and, despite improvements in the overall health of the population, there are troubling indicators that all is not well. On the plus side, education shows positive signs, community vitality is higher and engagement in the democratic process (i.e., voting) has risen. Yet Canadians' well-being has not kept pace with the recovery of the economy. A similar trend would also likely be shown in the United States, if an index of well-being were available there.

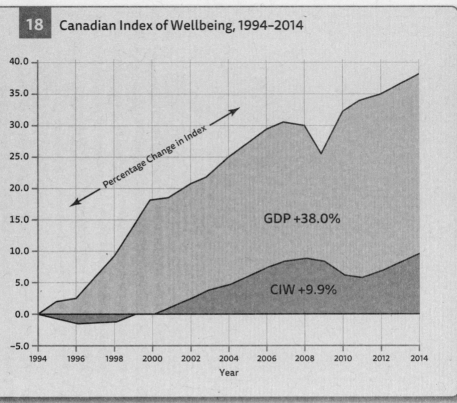

18 Canadian Index of Wellbeing, 1994–2014

SOURCE: The Canadian Index of Wellbeing, 2016. Accessible at uwaterloo.ca/canadian-index-wellbeing/sites/ca
.canadian-index-wellbeing/files/uploads/files/c011676-nationalreport-ciw_final-s.pdf.

Implementing the Canadian Index of Wellbeing has not been without its challenges. First, the CIW was developed by experts in their respective fields of study (health, education, economy, the environment) and not based on the new science of well-being or on the values of Canadians. Nor were the indicators vetted with Canadians in terms of whether they actually *measure what matters* to their well-being and quality of life. Experts often assume that the indicators they have chosen to measure well-being are objective and reflect measures of importance to Canadians.

Secondly, acceptance of the CIW has been a challenge; no federal, provincial or municipal government across Canada has officially adopted it as a measure of progress to guide policy or budgeting decisions. Ideally an index like the CIW would be used by all levels of government in Canada and other nations when preparing budgets and conducting strategic long-range planning. In my own work around strategic planning in Edmonton and Alberta, I have found that examining the interrelationships between GDP and other well-being metrics or indicators can be very useful. For example, as described earlier, I found strong correlations between GDP and the incidence of cancer in Alberta, which is not to imply a direct correlation between economic growth and the incidence of cancer per se. These kinds of correlations can be useful for planners and economists who try to forecast the impacts of changes in economic conditions, such as a drop in the price of oil in Alberta, and measures of societal well-being, including things like stress, domestic violence, safety and even environmental quality. I would also advocate a system of public well-being accounts, as described above.

Notes

1. careerfaqs.com.au/news/news-and-views/career-goals-you-should-tick-off-in-your-40s, accessed May 29, 2017.
2. David Cameron speech from May 2006 as reported in theguardian.com/politics/2006/may/22/conservatives.uk2, accessed May 29, 2017.
3. John Helliwell, Richard Layard and Jeffrey Sachs, eds., *World Happiness Report*, The Earth Institute, Columbia University, 2013; available at earth.columbia.edu/sitefiles/file/Sachs%20Writing/2012/World%20Happiness%20Report.pdf.
4. M. E. P. Seligman. *Flourish*. New York, NY: Simon & Schuster, 2011.
5. Personal communication with Karen Pheasant, September 15, 2016, Edmonton, Alberta.
6. sparknotes.com/philosophy/utilitarianism/summary.html.
7. Jeremy Bentham, J. H. Burns and H. L. A. Hart, eds. *A Comment on the Commentaries and A Fragment on Government*. London: The Athlone Press, 1977. p. 393. ISBN 0485132125.
8. John Stuart Mill. *Utilitarianism* (1 ed.). London: Parker, Son & Bourn, West Strand, 1863. Retrieved May 9, 2017, via Google Books.
9. *The Autobiography of Benjamin Franklin*, Touchstone (January 6, 2004), ISBN 9780-0-74325-506-6.
10. Robert D. McGarvey. *Futuromics: A Guide to Thriving in Capitalism's Third Wave*, 2016. Available in Kindle version on Amazon.com: amazon.com/Futuromics-Guide-Thriving-Capitalisms-Third-ebook/dp/B01J4UOFUC.
11. United Nations. Sustainable Development Goals. Available at sustainabledevelopment.un.org/?menu=1300 accessed May 30, 2017.

12. I use the original 13th-century Middle English definition of wealth as "the state, quality or condition (th) of well-being (wele)." This older definition of wealth also refers to "happiness" or "prosperity in abundance of possessions or riches."

13. dictionary.com/browse/capital

14. Deiner is an American psychologist, professor, and author; professor of psychology at the Universities of Utah and Virginia; Joseph R. Smiley Distinguished Professor Emeritus at the University of Illinois; as well as a senior scientist for the Gallup Organization.

15. Department for International Development. Sustainable Livelihoods Guidance Sheet: Introduction. 1999. livelihoods.org/info/info _guidancesheets.html#1.

16. John McArthur, with the Brookings Institute, suggests there are 300 million fewer people living in extreme poverty, or 650 million people living in extreme poverty conditions. See brookings.edu/blog/future -development/2017/06/01/how-many-countries-could-end-extreme -poverty-tomorrow/.

17. CIA World Factbook cia.gov/library/publications/the-world-factbook /geos/xx.html.

18. The cost would present only 0.26% of the combined GDP of the 10 richest countries in the world, 89.4% of the world's total GDP.

19. Edmonton living wage estimates for 2015 are based on the Edmonton Social Planning *Council Tracking the Trends*, 2015, p. 38.

CHAPTER 3

Bhutan, Edmonton and Alberta: Models of Well-Being Economies

EARLY ONE SATURDAY morning in September, 2011, I received an email from Prime Minister Jigme Thinley of Bhutan inviting me to a meeting in April of 2012 at the United Nations in New York. The purpose of the meeting was to discuss Bhutan's proposal to world leaders of adopting a new economic paradigm based on well-being and happiness. Bhutan, a tiny Buddhist kingdom with a population of more than 700,000, long ago adopted the model of Gross National Happiness to measure its economic progress as an alternative to GDP. The prime minister invited me to prepare a short policy paper expressing my vision for how Alberta and Canada might adopt well-being and happiness as a new economic paradigm.

The Royal Government of Bhutan brought together more than eight hundred distinguished participants at this meeting. They included United Nations Secretary-General Ban Ki-Moon, the president of the Republic of Costa Rica (Laura Chinchilla), Prince Charles (from London), the presidents of the UN General Assembly and Economic and Social Council, the administrator of the United Nations Development Program, government ministers and diplomats from around the world, leading economists such as Joseph Stiglitz, Jeffrey Sachs, John Helliwell and positive psychologist Martin Seligman, as well as various Nobel laureates, media and leaders of civil society, business and spirituality. I was disappointed that Canada was not represented by Prime Minister Harper or any other senior officials. After all, it was Canadian

19   Bhutan's Gross National Happiness Indicators and Accounting System

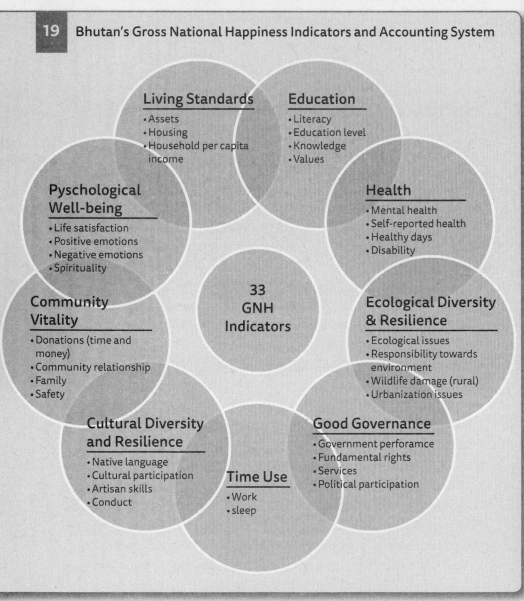

Living Standards
- Assets
- Housing
- Household per capita income

Education
- Literacy
- Education level
- Knowledge
- Values

Pyschological Well-being
- Life satisfaction
- Positive emotions
- Negative emotions
- Spirituality

Health
- Mental health
- Self-reported health
- Healthy days
- Disability

33 GNH Indicators

Community Vitality
- Donations (time and money)
- Community relationship
- Family
- Safety

Ecological Diversity & Resilience
- Ecological issues
- Responsibility towards environment
- Wildlife damage (rural)
- Urbanization issues

Cultural Diversity and Resilience
- Native language
- Cultural participation
- Artisan skills
- Conduct

Time Use
- Work
- sleep

Good Governance
- Government perforamce
- Fundamental rights
- Services
- Political participation

SOURCE: Kingdom of Bhutan; Gross National Happiness Centre.

researchers, including epidemiologist Michael Pennock, who had contributed to the development of Bhutan's Gross National Happiness Indicators and Accounting System (see Figure 19), which in turn had been inspired by the Canadian Index of Wellbeing (CIW).

On the morning of the meeting at breakfast, I met a Buddhist monk, the senior Buddhist adviser to the king of Thailand. We spoke about the Buddhist understanding of happiness, *sukha* (a Sanskrit word for happiness, ease, or bliss), which was always in balance with *dukkha* (suffering, stress and disappointment).[1] As we laughed about the limits of words and language, his friend, Tibetan Buddhist monk Matthieu Ricard, a French former molecular geneticist, joined us. We were oblivious to presence of the president of Costa Rica, Laura Chinchilla, who was having breakfast at the next table. These monks presented a Buddhist perspective on happiness and well-being at the UN meeting that day.

In the UN grand meeting hall were Charles Eisenstein, author of *Sacred Economics* (2011), and Helena Norberg-Hodge, producer and co-director of the documentary film *The Economics of Happiness* (2011).[2] We listened intently as dignitaries spoke about the importance of adopting Bhutan's proposed economic paradigm. One thing Charles and I agreed on was that no speakers made mention of the greatest barrier to the pursuit of authentic happiness. The elephant in the room was the world's debt-money system, with the burden of interest costs hidden in the cost of living. I mused that it would have been interesting to have held this high-level meeting so close to the money world of Wall Street without the presence of investment bankers to consider the merits of a well-being economy. There seemed to be a genuine commitment and enthusiasm amongst the participants that day to return to our own countries and communities to introduce the concepts into our respective worlds.

The second day of the UN high-level meetings entailed working sessions that explored some practical actions that could be taken to advance the new economic paradigm. I joined the civil society working session, made up of religious and civil society leaders across many faiths. I suggested in these sessions that what was required in addition to a functional well-being-based governance system was reforms in monetary policy, banking and investment that would align with nations' well-being objectives. Indeed, without redesigning money systems to support a paradigm shift to a new economy of well-being, it is likely that the shift would be drowned out by demands for more economic growth and more materialism driven by a rising tide of unpayable debts. In my proposal to Prime Minister Thinley I made the following points about such economic reform:

> I believe that at the heart of the failure of capitalism to improve the well-being conditions of humanity is the failure to understand the nature of money, the impact of fractional reserve banking on the destruction of natural, human and social capital, and the significant impact of usury (charging interest on money created) on the destruction of the human spirit. The world is currently stuck in a debt crisis primarily because it cannot imagine a system of money creation without debt-money. Indeed 97% or more of the world's money is created as debt (e.g., through loans by banks), which ultimately threatens the pursuit of genuine happiness and destroys the human spirit and hope.
>
> I believe that the pursuit of a sustainable, resilient and flourishing economy is possible only with a fundamental restructuring of the world's financial systems where money would be created not as debt-money but aligned with genuine wealth, well-being and happiness. I have proposed and designed a new monetary system that I recently presented to ethical bankers and captains of capitalism.

It is possible to develop the monetary system that Abraham Lincoln envisioned. Lincoln stated clearly, "The Government should create, issue, and circulate all the currency and credits needed to satisfy the spending power of the Government and the buying power of consumers. By the adoption of these principles, the taxpayers will be saved immense sums of interest. Money will cease to be master and become the servant of humanity."[3]

And so it was that on April 2, 2012, a global movement was launched to advance a new economic paradigm based on well-being and happiness. March 20 was established as International Day of Happiness. The key conditions for the new economy of well-being would include

+ ecological sustainability;
+ fair distribution of income and wealth;

⬧ the efficient use of resources, and;

⬧ a healthy balance among thriving natural, human, social, cultural, and built assets.

Prime Minister Thinley encouraged us to return home and become ambassadors in our nations and communities for this new economic paradigm.

While sitting in the UN session, I received an invitation from RT (Russian Television) to join their premier policy talk show, *CrossTalk*, to discuss the merits of measuring happiness with host Peter Lavelle.[4] In the interview—which took place in an Edmonton TV studio following my return from New York—I debated the practical aspects of incorporating measures of happiness and well-being into the current economic measures of progress and decision-making with two London-based economists.

Back to Edmonton: The City That Could

I returned to my home in Edmonton, Alberta, enthused about advancing the new economic paradigm in my own city. Edmonton had already shown leadership in adopting in 2009 the 50-well-being indicator Genuine Progress Index (GPI) as a measure of progress for its ten-year strategic plan called *The Way Ahead*.

The morning after my return from New York, the host of Edmonton's CBC (Canadian Broadcasting Service) morning radio show, Lydia Neufeld, invited me to speak about my trip. I noted that Edmonton was already well on its way in adopting Bhutan's proposal with a commitment to the Edmonton GPI, measuring progress in terms of what really matters to the well-being of Edmontonians.

I was particularly enthused about the prospect that Edmonton could take the next step of incorporating well-being impacts into its policies, programs and annual operating and capital budgets. For me, this was the decisive frontier. The ultimate goal of civic governments would be to demonstrate the well-being impacts of taxes within an integrated five-capital asset balance sheet. The onus would be on ensuring the highest and best use of the city's community assets (people, relationships, lands, the environment, built infrastructure and financial wealth) to deliver the highest possible well-being for the greatest number of Edmontonians.

Emboldened with this vision, I was invited a few days later by one of Edmonton's city councilors to speak about the merits of maintaining Edmonton's commitment to the GPI or well-being index. In my presentation to Mayor Stephen Mandel and city council, I noted that Edmonton was well positioned to become a global leader amongst municipal governments in practically advancing a new economic well-being paradigm, exceeding even Bhutan's current progress.

To my dismay, the mayor and the city's chief financial officer failed to grasp the value of adopting such a paradigm and voted against a small budget that would have updated the Edmonton GPI in future. Their rationale seemed to be based on the anxiety of accountability; accepting a broad societal well-being index might imply to citizens a direct link to city programs, services and budgets.

The experience with Edmonton has shown me the importance of patience and perseverance; the approach to governance based on well-being may seem common sense, but we clearly have a long way to go in demonstrating the utility of such a paradigm shift.

The Promise of Alberta

Alberta is one the richest provinces in Canada, with an abundance of natural, human and social human assets. It benefits from the natural beauty of the Rocky Mountains (including Banff and Jasper National Parks), fertile agricultural lands, abundant fresh water, healthy watersheds and the second-largest oil reserves in the world. Alberta is a young province, founded in 1905, settled by immigrants from around the world, and ancestral home to a diverse and vibrant culture of Indigenous peoples (Plains and Woodland Cree, Blackfoot, Tsuu T'ina, Plains Ojibwa [Anishinabe], Nakoda, Dene, Tasttine, and Inuit), who have lived here for more than ten thousand years. Albertans are known for their entrepreneurial and resilient spirit and warm hearts; we are a welcoming people rich in relationships and social capital. We have a strong sense of belonging. We also enjoy the highest levels of GDP and household income per capita amongst Canadian provinces, which is both a blessing and a challenge. We are materially rich but at times experience higher levels of depression and suicide than other, less economically prosperous provinces. We have at times become complacent and entitled, expecting the benefits of abundant oil riches to continue forever. We are reminded that market cycles can quickly derail and dash our pursuit of happiness. Yet I believe that Alberta is one of the best places in the world to advance a new economic paradigm of well-being, no matter who leads the province politically.

Alberta has been the home of long-term, one-party political dynasties. The Alberta Social Credit party, founded by a charismatic Christian preacher, Bill Aberhart, governed the province from 1935 to 1971. As premier, Aberhart led the province through the Great Depression, instituting anti-poverty and debt relief programs and other governmental reforms as well the conservation of natural resources. His attempts to introduce banking reforms, including the creation of Alberta's own currency, met with less success, opposed by the federal government in Ottawa and Toronto bankers. Yet his most important legacy endures: the Alberta Treasury Branch, North America's largest public bank.

In 1971, a young new leader of the Progressive Conservative party, Peter Lougheed, swept to power, wiping out the Social Credit party. The PCs ruled Alberta for the next 44 years, until 2015. Lougheed was fortunate in riding a wave of rising oil prices, caused by the 1973 OPEC oil crisis, that sustained Alberta's economic prosperity for the next 42 years, until they collapsed in 2015. He brought in new economic policy ideas, including the establishment of Alberta's oil and gas heritage savings and trust fund—one of the world's first sovereign wealth funds. Lougheed developed his economic vision in a policy white paper that set the stage for the remarkable economic progress that has made Alberta a model of economic growth.

In 2015, the Progressive Conservative dynasty ended as abruptly as the Social Credit one had 44 years earlier. Led by Rachel Notley, the daughter of Lougheed's longtime opponent Grant Notley, the left-leaning New Democratic Party won a landslide victory soon called the Orange Crush, in reference to the party's colors.

Albertans seemed ready for a new government and tired of the old ruling elites. Unfortunately, Notley's victory came at the worst possible time; world oil prices were collapsing and Alberta's financial house was falling into disorder. A province that had enjoyed regular budget surpluses was suddenly faced with a $10-billion budget deficit, and both GDP and material well-being were hit hard. Unemployment soared in Alberta's oil patch. Governments rise and fall based on economic conditions; people tend to blame the governing party for economic malaise and reward them when the economy is vibrant.

Is Alberta's crisis an opportunity to advance a new economic paradigm based on well-being? I believe so. The Chinese symbol for crisis is *wēijī*, which means "incipient moment; crucial point, when something begins or changes." *Wēijī* indicates a perilous situation when one should be especially wary. Is this Alberta's *wēijī*, an important tipping point or fork in the road, the time for a paradigm shift and a new pathway of economic well-being?

wēi   jī

It is not only Alberta but the entire world that stands at the tipping point of systemic crisis: financial, institutional, climatic, and ethical. Politicians are reluctant to take on new economic policies and ideas that stray too far from public acceptance or their own party ideologies. Yet pursuing a moderate economic paradigm and the middle path that an economy of well-being suggests would surely capture the hearts of Albertans and all Canadians. But to my knowledge, no political party in Canada at any level of government has yet considered an economy of well-being policy platform.

I believe Alberta is in prime position to advance a new economic model, especially during this time of economic crisis. Here is what I would propose to Premier Notley and to any provincial or federal political parties.

First, that the province of Alberta would establish a new economic policy that would make well-being the highest aspiration for progress. (See Figure 20 for the proposed structure of the model.)

Alberta's mission statement might read as follows:

The Alberta government exists to serve the best interests of all Albertans; to maintain or improve the well-being conditions of all Albertans and Alberta's assets.

This mission would be supported by a common set of values created by Albertans, defining what makes life worthwhile to them. The mission and values would be built upon a five-year strategic business plan, with goals, strategies, budgets and progress indicators such as an Alberta Well-Being Index and well-being indicators drawn from Alberta's new set of integrated five-asset accounts. A budgeting and reporting system would be required to report on the state of well-being and progress being made toward the aspiration of the mission statement.

Second, that all government policies, programs, services and budgets would be oriented toward improving well-being conditions across the province, in all sectors of the economy and households, regardless of income, gender, religion or location.

Third, that provincial and federal governments would adopt a new public accounting system that is based on a comprehensive and complete accounting of the five assets of the nation or community: human, social, natural, built and financial assets. Without such an accounting, it's impossible to know whether an economy is on a sustainable, resilient path.

Fourth, accountability for value of taxes and public programs would demonstrate a measurable well-being return on investment through full-cost-accounting protocols applied to all programs and services. An onus on well-being impact and full-cost accounting for all public policies and programs would change the very nature of public sector budgeting and accountability and

20 A Well-Being Economy Model for Governments

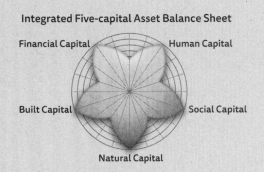

Integrated Five-capital Asset Balance Sheet

Financial Capital   Human Capital

Built Capital   Social Capital

Natural Capital

Mission:
To maintain or improve well-being conditions for both people and nature.

Values:
What we value most about life

──── Domains of Well-being ────

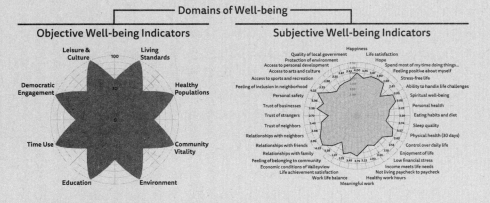

Objective Well-being Indicators

Leisure & Culture   Living Standards
Democratic Engagement   Healthy Populations
Time Use   Community Vitality
Education   Environment

Subjective Well-being Indicators

SOURCE: Anielski Management Inc. 2017.

help citizens understand the value they receive from the taxes they pay.

Fifth, I would urge the Bank of Canada, the Canadian Pension Plan and provincial sovereign wealth funds (such as Alberta's AIMCo and the Alberta Heritage Savings and Trust Fund) and public banks (Alberta Treasury Brand being the only provincial public bank in Canada) to orient their policies toward building and sustaining the five strategic assets of the nation or provinces using a proper public asset balance sheet to guide decisions.

This is what I would advise any Canadian premier or prime minister, as well as caucuses, treasury boards and finance ministers. If I were the finance minister of Alberta and head of the treasury board, I would immediately ask for a comprehensive inventory of all the province's assets. I would begin by completing a traditional financial audit and assessment of the physical, qualitative and monetary/economic conditions of all of Alberta's abundant assets. This would be similar to a financial audit and inventory conducted by accounting firms for enterprises. Then I would conduct a public asset inventory and assessment of the well-being conditions of Alberta's human and social assets in all our cities, towns and Indigenous communities (First Nations and Métis), which would include an assessment of the health (emotional, physical, mental, spiritual), happiness, life satisfaction, trust, relationships, financial fitness and resiliency, sense of belonging, personal safety, hope, education, skills, competencies and the other myriad human and social assets of every community. I would ask for a full accounting of Alberta's labor force and levels of underemployment, and the skill sets that will be necessary to build the assets that will fuel the new economy of well-being. This assessment would guide high school curriculums and post-secondary investments in universities and colleges.

I would ask for a complete accounting of the physical quantity and value of the non-renewable oil, gas, coal and mineral reserves in the province, as well as their remaining reserve-life. In this analysis I would want a forensic and regular accounting of the returns on investment Albertans receive in the form of royalties and savings from the extraction of the oil, gas and coal assets. If this were done, we could be confident that Albertans were receiving their fair share of their common natural resource wealth. In addition, I would ask for an assessment of Alberta's renewable energy capacity: wind, solar, hydro, geothermal and biomass. I would ask for a detailed renewable energy strategy that charted a sustainable energy and financial future optimizing returns on declining oil and gas resources while optimizing renewable energy opportunities. In addition, I would ask for an audit of the ecological health and state of Alberta's watersheds, agricultural lands, forests, carbon and ecosystem services, plus a true accounting of the unfunded ecological liabilities (including carbon) that constitute a risk both to nature and Alberta's future generations.

An assessment of Alberta's social and cultural assets would survey Albertans about their sense of relationships, belonging and trust within the communities they live in, toward neighbors, local businesses and elected officials. The strength of Alberta's social capital is our comparative advantage in an economy of well-being.

A comprehensive built capital asset account would show the state, value and replacement cost of Alberta's infrastructure: roads, bridges, trails, rail lines, pipelines, electrical infrastructure, hospitals and other buildings and equipment. I would ask for each built asset class to be evaluated in the same way real estate assets are currently assessed, that is, in terms of their highest and best use. No longer should finance ministers be surprised by unfunded infrastructure liabilities with a proper accounting of the utility of infrastructure and the need for regular maintenance and replacement schedules. This should be no different from how I manage our own household assets; I regularly calculate the life and replacement value of all aspects of our 1909 home—the furnace, roof, appliances—and our car, setting aside the appropriate asset replacement funds each month to replace those assets at the end of their life. Imagine if all governments established similar asset replacement contingency funds!

Finally, as finance minister I would ask for a comprehensive financial assets assessment. This would include assets that reside in Alberta's public bank, ATB (Alberta Treasury Branch) Financial, and AIMCo (Alberta Investment Management Corp.). Today you will find roughly $47 billion and $95.7 billion of available financial capital assets in these respective public financial institutions. I would ask the heads of these institutions how they can help leverage and finance the development of Alberta's asset potential to build the new economy of well-being.

The result would be a proper balance sheet for the province of Alberta. The finance minister will learn, as I have as a new member of the Alberta Provincial Audit Committee, that Alberta, like other provinces, lacks a proper balance sheet of all assets. I have asked the Alberta auditor general why this is true. He directed my question to the Public Sector Accounting Handbook, which provides no answers.

From a macro-economic policy perspective related to trade of comparative advantages of assets between provinces and with other world economies, I am of the opinion, similar to that of Adam Smith proposed in *The Wealth of Nations*, that trade economics should be based on the exchange of relative comparative asset advantage, namely, exchange of surplus or excess over meeting domestic needs. Smith showed how both parties can benefit from trade, but it was David Ricardo who is credited with what is commonly called "comparative advantage": the idea that both parties can benefit from trade even if one of them is better at producing everything than the other.[5] In my opinion, the notion of comparative advantage (where trade is driven by the differences between two jurisdictions and the opportunity for each jurisdiction to specialize in what it does most effectively) and natural advantage (based on unique natural capital assets and ecosystems) can be strengthened with a broader five-asset model of exchange, where the goal is to improve the state of well-being of all trading partners. This would require a careful accounting of total assets, their life-expectancy and value, to ensure that domestic well-being and self-sufficiency are assured before entering into inter-provincial or other trading relationships with different or comparable assets. Free trade of comparative asset advantages would thus entail optimizing well-being conditions and sustainable asset optimization across large-scale ecosystems (e.g., watersheds) and countries. The current free-trade regime that has dominated world trade since the 1970s would most likely be shown to be inefficient in terms of both energy and effort in the exchange of goods and services. An international trade regime based on optimizing well-being would fundamentally change the nature of trade in ways that Adam Smith could not have imagined.

Alberta's Preliminary Asset Accounts

Alberta's natural assets are significant in both aggregate and on a per capita basis. Alberta is blessed with a land base of 66 million hectares, more than 1.86 times the size of Germany yet with only 5% of that country's population. Alberta's massive energy resources include the second-largest oil reserves on the planet

(168 billion barrels of oil sands) that, valued at a conservative
US$40/bbl., would be worth $8.2 trillion. At current rates of production Alberta's massive oil sands would last at least 215 years;
and this is using very conservative reserve figures.

At the same time, Alberta has superb renewable energy capacity. With 1.5 times more sunshine hours than Germany and
almost twice the land base, the province's photovoltaic (solar)
electricity potential is enormous. Yet Alberta currently has only
about 17 MW of installed solar PV systems, while Germany has
more than 40,000 MW. On a per capita basis, Germany has 208
times more installed PV solar than Alberta (0.50 kW/capita for
Germany versus 0.0024 kW/capita for Alberta).

Alberta could invest $15 billion over the next ten years to in-
stall the full potential of solar PV arrays on one million homes,
making the province self-sufficient in renewable electricity. Alberta would even surpass renewable energy leaders like Germany.
Such an investment would ensure that each Alberta household
would become energy self-sufficient. Not only is this financially
and economically attractive it would also deliver a positive well-
being return on investment, lowering health care costs by improving the air quality, which is still marred by coal-fired electricity.
Making a well-being case for such a capital investment is rather
straightforward.

Alberta also incurs significant unfunded environmental liabilities upon the rest of the planet. For example, Alberta emitted
about 274 Mt of CO_2 in 2016, or about 38% of Canada's total carbon
emissions. A proper Alberta natural capital balance sheet would
show the societal cost of the province's carbon emissions and the
damages they cause to ecosystem health, which I've estimated at
$13.7 billion per annum using Canada's national carbon price of
$50/t CO_2. None of these environmental liabilities appears on Al-
berta's books or the books of Alberta's energy companies. Moreover, both reinsurance and insurance companies that provide
policies to these energy companies do not include these costs in
their premiums.

Alberta's natural capital balance sheet would show the rate of
return on Alberta's oil, gas, coal and other natural assets in the

form of royalties paid by industry to governments. This would ask the fundamental question: Did Alberta receive the highest possible return on its natural capital assets from industry in the form of royalties and other taxes? In a historical analysis of Alberta's record of royalty collection since 1971, I have shown that the royalties collected by the government for every dollar of oil and gas produced and sold have been declining since the early 1990s (Figure 21). Based on both Alberta government budget projections and oil industry production forecasts, 2017 will represent the lowest level of oil rent collection in Alberta's history, falling to an estimated 3.6% of the value of projected oil and gas revenues by industry. This steady decline in the share of oil and gas sales passed on to Albertans is troubling, since it means that billions of dollars in royalties have disappeared and were not otherwise invested in Alberta's trust funds. I have estimated that, had

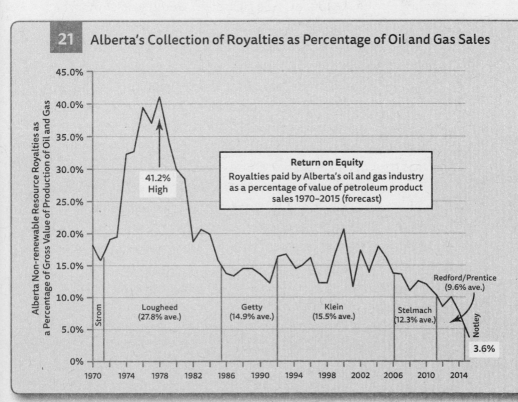

21   **Alberta's Collection of Royalties as Percentage of Oil and Gas Sales**

SOURCE: Prepared by Mark Anielski (Anielski Management Inc.) based on Alberta government public accounts (non-renewable resource royalties) various years and petroleum resource sale statistics from the Canadian Association of Petroleum Producers (CAPP) Statistical Handbook, various years.

Albertans received the same average rate of return in royalties as Premier Peter Lougheed collected between 1971 and 1985 (27 cents per dollar of oil and gas sales), Albertans would now have a savings fund of well over $500 billion, if not close to Norway's $900-billion government fund (formally the Petroleum Fund), which was modelled after Alberta's.

The Alberta balance sheet for human and social capital would provide a complete inventory of Alberta's population and demographics, including a profile of health (mental, physical, emotional and spiritual), work satisfaction, financial well-being, living-wage analysis and education levels and skills, as well as perceptions of happiness, hope, relationships and trust. Alberta's human and social capital assets would be significant, in the form of the value of a skilled workforce, a healthy and young population, relatively happy people, and a strong sense of belonging or strong relational capital. The assessment would also show what Albertans love most about Alberta, why they came here, and why they choose to stay, whether Albertans enjoy their work and whether they feel their lives are meaningful.

This inventory of human capital assets would include an annual subjective well-being survey of Albertans in which all citizens can self-assess their personal state of well-being. This would include their self-assessment of life satisfaction, the meaningfulness they derive from work and even the hope they have for the future. This accounting of the social capital of the province would consider questions to all people about their sense of belonging to communities and their sense of trust in politicians, local businesses and others in society. Understanding how connected Albertans feel to their communities is an important accounting of social capital. I believe that trust is perhaps the most precious asset of all. Without trust you have the potential for societal breakdown. Fortunately, many Albertans have a high sense of belonging to their neighborhoods.

In terms of life satisfaction, Albertans ranked sixth in Canada in overall life satisfaction in 2014 according to Statistics Canada, with over 92% of them feeling satisfied or very satisfied with life. Alberta ranked behind top-ranked Saskatchewan and second-ranked Prince Edward Island, with Ontario and Nunavut at the bottom. However, in the most recent (2016) national happiness poll by Angus Reid, only 80% of Albertans said they were very happy or pretty happy with life; 17% said they are "not too happy."[6] One could say that Albertans remain bullish about life, despite a significant 61% drop in oil prices since 2013 and a sharp rise in the province's unemployment rate, from 4.6% in 2013 to 8.4% in March 2017.[7] Research shows that nothing detracts from well-being and happiness more than being unemployed.

On the darker side of Alberta's human capital balance sheet is rising anxiety and falling mental well-being; suicides are on the rise. Statistics show that for each 1% rise in the unemployment rate, the rate of suicide increases by 0.79%. Alberta's medical examiner projected that suicides would increase by 30% in 2015 compared to 2014. Statistics for the first six months of 2015 counted 327 suicides compared to historical annual provincial rates of 500 to 550. More people commit suicide in Alberta than are killed in car crashes (about 350 fatalities per year). This trend appears to be a direct result of the collapse in world oil prices that has led to sharp rises in unemployment.

How could Alberta ensure its long-term financial sustainability in spite of the current downturn in global oil prices? By making use of North America's most important financial assets, ATB Financial and AIMCo, with combined assets of $140 billion. ATB Financial is North America's largest public bank, with over $47 billion in assets. Having a public bank provides Alberta with unique advantages: it can lend money both to Albertans and to the Alberta government at rates much lower than commercial banks. Moreover, ATB is 100% owned by the people of Alberta and is 100% backed by the assets of the province, even if these assets are not fully accounted for. Because ATB is owned by Albertans, the Alberta government could direct ATB to provide at-cost or near-zero interest loans to develop, for example, Alberta's amazing renewable energy capacity, help some of the thousands of unemployed skilled Albertans to start viable small businesses, provide zero-interest student loans or finance affordable housing assets with zero-interest mortgages, like Habitat for Humanity currently does in Edmonton. I will speak about these opportunities later.

I believe Alberta is ideally situated to develop the first working model of an economy of well-being. The province could advance a new economic vision based on the notion that improving and sustaining well-being conditions of Albertans is a central objective of government. There is a fundamental difference between the pursuit of pure economic growth measured by a single indicator (GDP) and well-being, measured in terms of what matters most to the quality of life of Albertans. Making well-being impacts the fundamental focus of Alberta government policies and programs will provide the government with the capacity to report on the value Albertans receive from taxes and other revenues.

I believe the economic crisis presents a perfect opportunity for Albertans to step back and take stock of the new opportunities that present themselves in the eye of this economic storm. Alberta has an important opportunity to advance the new economic paradigm of well-being, building on its natural advantages and abundant and vibrant human, social and natural assets.

Notes

1. The Buddha taught that the stress and disappointment in life (dukkha) come from craving and grasping; at the root of craving and grasping is ignorance.
2. Many people have asked if Norberg-Hodge's film was based on my 2007 book *The Economics of Happiness*. There is no relationship between my book and her film. The subject of her film is economic globalization and how it has negatively impacted many cultures (e.g., Ladakh in India) and her promotion of greater localization.
3. Quoted on the Money Masters website [online]. [cited February 15, 2018] www.themoneymasters.com/the-money-masters-famous -quotations-on-banking/.
4. The April 5, 2012, airing of the *CrossTalk* program can be found at youtu.be/8hqM8gD9k2A. Accessed June 1, 2017.
5. Adam Smith. *An Inquiry into the Nature and Causes of the Wealth of Nations* (1789; 1st edition 1776) Book IV, Chapter 3, paragraph 31.
6. Angus Reid Institute. 2016. As reported at cbc.ca/news/canada /canadians-happy-survey-1.3406124 accessed May 30, 2017.
7. Statistics Canada, CANSIM, table 282-0087 Labour Force Characteristics. statcan.gc.ca/tables-tableaux/sum-som/l01/cst01/lfss01c-eng .htm. Accessed May 30, 2017.

CHAPTER 4

The Well-Being Community

MEASURING THE WELL-BEING of a community means measuring what matters most to the quality of life and values of that community. I have been working on the development of community well-being measurement and reporting systems since 1999, including
  ◆ The Edmonton Social Health Index (1999)
  ◆ The US Genuine Progress Indicator (1999)
  ◆ The Alberta Genuine Progress Indicator (2001)
  ◆ The Canadian Index of Wellbeing (2002–12)
  ◆ China's Xiaokang (Well-Being) Society Indicators for China's Municipalities (2005)
  ◆ The City of Leduc (Alberta) Well-Being Index (2006)
  ◆ The City of Santa Monica (California) Sustainable Well-Being Index (2007)
  ◆ Innsbruck (Austria) Well-Being Indicators (2008)
  ◆ The City of Edmonton (Alberta) Well-Being Index (2009)
  ◆ The Town of Olds (Alberta) Well-Being Index (2013)
  ◆ The Town of Valleyview (Alberta) Well-Being Index (2017)
  ◆ The Commune of Arue (Tahiti) (2017)

The Edmonton Social Health Index

My earliest work in measuring community well-being was in 1999, when I developed the Edmonton Social Health Index (ESHI) for the Edmonton Social Planning Council.[1] The ESHI is a composite measure of personal, family and community well-being composed of 22 well-being indicators (see Table 4) and organized into five themes: a) population health, b) personal and family stability,

TABLE 4: Edmonton Social Health Index Indicators

Population Health
1.   Life Expectancy
2.   Sexually Transmitted Infections
3.   Low Birth-Weight Babies
4.   Infant Mortality

Personal & Family Stability
5.   Teen Birth Rate
6.   Child & Family Services Caseloads
7.   Suicide
8.   Divorced / Separated Families

Financial Security
9.   Median Family Income
10. Insolvency Rate
11. Percentage of Persons in Families Below LIM
12. Percentage of Children in Families Below LIM
13. Depth of Poverty
14. Average Cost of two-bedroom apartment
15. Food Bank Use
16. High School Not Completed
17. Post-Secondary Educational Attainment
18. Unemployment

Community Safety
19. Property Crime Rate
20. Violent Crime Rate

Participation & Environment
21. Commuting by Transit, Bike or Walking
22. Voter Turnout

---

c) financial security, d) community safety and e) participation and environment. Raw statistical data for each indicator is converted to a 100-point index system (100 points meaning the best possible condition of well-being). This allows for visual comparison of various indicators, showing trends over time; for example, GDP per capita trends can be compared with life expectancy, household income or suicide trends.

The 22 well-being indicators are given equal weight in a com-

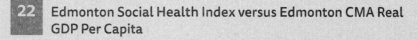

22 Edmonton Social Health Index versus Edmonton CMA Real GDP Per Capita

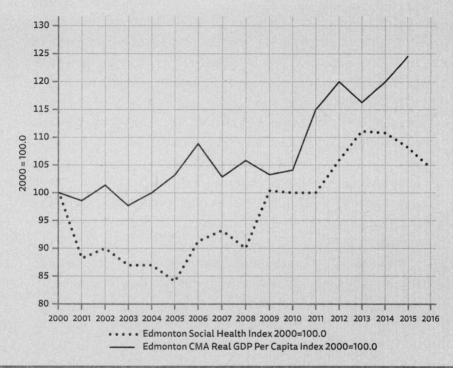

• • • • • Edmonton Social Health Index 2000=100.0

—————— Edmonton CMA Real GDP Per Capita Index 2000=100.0

SOURCE: Edmonton Social Health Index is from Tracking the Trends 2016; Edmonton CMA GDP figures are from Statistics Canada CANSIM 381–5000 and 381–0036 and Edmonton CMA population figures from CANSIM 051–0056.

posite Social Health Index of wellbeing. Figure 22 shows Edmonton's ESHI contrasted with Edmonton's real GDP per capita, using the year 2000 as the base year for the period 2000–16.

The picture shows a positive trend; in spite of some negative trends in real GDP, Edmonton's overall state of well-being has been improving since 2000. This seems to suggest that the Edmonton community remains resilient despite economic shocks that also affected Calgary and other parts of the province dependent on the oil and gas sector. Key indicators that have shown positive improvements in Edmonton include rising real median household income, decreasing unemployment rates, fewer people living in poverty, fewer households using the foodbank and falling property and violent crime rates.

The Edmonton SHI work was, in part, my inspiration for a more comprehensive assessment of well-being and sustainability for the City of Leduc, Alberta, which I completed in 2006 and discussed in my first book, *The Economics of Happiness*. Leduc has maintained a commitment to the five-asset model of genuine wealth with annual engagements with citizens to reaffirm the values and issues of well-being important to this growing Alberta city.

The most promising aspect of the Leduc experience was working with Dominic Mishio, who I first met at the launch of the Leduc Genuine Wealth and Well-Being Project in 2006. Dominic, then only 20 years of age, was so captured by the project that he asked me to be his mentor. At first I was reluctant, but I grew to appreciate the value of our conversations, which focused on the practical political and governance aspects of the well-being economic model.

Dominic aspired to becoming like Robert Kennedy, his political hero. He explained that is was because of the foresight of Leduc leaders in conducting a well-being assessment of his community that he chose to continue living there, though he, like other youth, was drawn to the big city life. Moreover, he chose to run for city council in 2007, securing a seat and becoming Alberta's youngest elected official.

Dominic would win a second term in 2010 and go on to serve as deputy mayor during his two terms on municipal council. I challenged him to think about every policy and budget decision from the perspective of the well-being impact (return) on investment of taxes, operating and capital expenditures. I convinced Dominic that taking such an approach to decision-making would change the nature of the conversation on council and indeed could become a model for other communities in Canada and the United States: a well-being approach to planning, budgeting and governance of municipalities and even nations. Dominic was keen about linking budget decisions to demonstrating well-being impacts and thus showing genuine value for taxpayer dollars. At last, I had found a politician who grasped the value of a well-being economic paradigm. In 2013 Dominic Mishio was invited to leave Alberta and move to Toronto to become the Canada Country Director for the Global Poverty and Global Citizen initiative, funded by the Bill and Melinda Gates Foundation, with offices in Toronto and New York. My hope is that Dominic will continue to be an advocate for the new economy of well-being.

Measuring the Well-Being of Valleyview, Alberta

In 2016 I was invited by Marty Paradine, the town manager for the northern Alberta town of Valleyview, to conduct an asset and well-being assessment for this community of 1,900 people. I was joined by a new colleague, Ian McCormack, a specialist in municipal governance, to complete the work within 18 months. Marty, an engineer, was intrigued with developing a new integrated asset management system for municipal governments with a well-being focus. In May of 2017, the results of both an objective and subjective assessment of community well-being were completed, including a subjective well-being survey of the community. A remarkable 15% of citizens participated in the survey, along with the entire population of Grade 6 school children.

The goal of the assessment was to provide a baseline for well-being conditions in Valleyview, including asking citizens what they like most about their communities and what things they would improve, both in the life of the community and their personal lives. We also asked them about their perceptions of happiness, life satisfaction, standards of living, health (including mental, spiritual and physical health), work satisfaction, life-time balance, feelings of belonging and trust of neighbors, local businesses and strangers, perceptions of safety, access to arts, culture, recreation and personal development, the integrity of local government and their ratings of municipal government services and amenities. I used Bhutan's Gross National Happiness model and the Canadian Index of Wellbeing model (which is similar to Bhutan's GNH) as a framework for measuring well-being across eight domains.

TABLE 5: Valleyview (Alberta) Subjective Well-Being Index, 2017

	Valleyview Index (out of 100 points)
Personal Well-Being and Life-Satisfaction Index	70.0
Material and Financial Well-Being Index	62.0
Work-Life Balance Index	70.0
Workplace Well-Being Index	75.0
Neighborhood Well-Being Index	72.0
Cultural Well-Being Index	63.0
Governance Index	69.0
Environment Well-Being Index	67.0
Valleyview Well-Being Index	69.0

SOURCE: Town of Valleyview Well-Being Assessment, 2017. Completed by Anielski Management Inc and Strategic Steps Inc.

Table 5 summarizes the survey results into eight well-being domains using a scale of 0 to 100, derived from a community-wide well-being survey conducted over a six-week period. The well-being scores will provide different organizations in Valleyview (e.g., the chamber of commerce, schools, the police and food banks) as well as citizens with a baseline of the state of well-being of their community.

The results of the subjective well-being survey are presented in the form of a spider-graphic with an image of a flower water-marked on the index. The flower is a good way to represent the flourishing of key attributes of well-being, including happiness, health, diet, sleep, spiritual well-being, work–life balance, workplace well-being, relationships and trust of others, sufficient financial resources, healthy democracy and environmental protection. In addition, citizens were asked to describe what they love about their community, identify their unique gifts and skills (personal assets) that they would like to share with others in the community, describe what areas in their personal life they would like to improve and say what amenities in the community they would like to see improve to increase overall quality of life.

Some of the most interesting findings in the assessment of Valleyview's state of well-being were the perceptions of financial

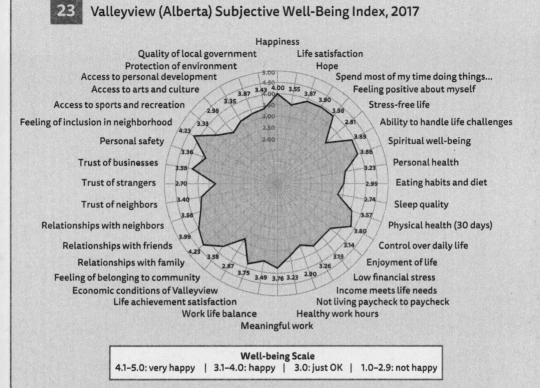

23 Valleyview (Alberta) Subjective Well-Being Index, 2017

Well-being Scale
4.1–5.0: very happy | 3.1–4.0: happy | 3.0: just OK | 1.0–2.9: not happy

SOURCE: Town of Valleyview Well-Being Assessment, 2017. Completed by Anielski Management Inc and Strategic Steps Inc.

stress in relationship to real income data. Based on Statistics Canada household income statistics, I estimated that 44% of households in Vallyeview were living below a living wage, while an estimated 9.8% were below the poverty line (roughly $36,000 household income for a family of four). A living wage for a family of four is estimated at $62,690, or roughly $16.50 per hour per working adult. In direct contrast, the well-being survey found that only 49% of adults felt their current level of income was sufficient to meet their current life needs, 43% experienced a lot of stress in their lives and 38% said they were living paycheck to paycheck.

In terms of happiness, 82% of adults surveyed felt either happy or very happy with life and 73% were satisfied. Roughly 83% were hopeful about the future, with Grade 6 students being slightly happier and more hopeful than adults. Roughly 77% of adults said that for the most part they spend time doing things they enjoy. Still, the fact that 4.8% of adults feel unhappy with life, 4.8% of adults are unhopeful and 9.1% are unsatisfied with life means there is room for improvement.

What I found particularly hopeful was that the Grade 6 student population were happy and hopeful about their future. Over 85% of all Grade 6 students feel happy or very happy about life, and over 82% feel hopeful about the future. More promising is that roughly half of the Grade 6 students in the Valleyview school district live in the Sturgeon Lake First Nation Cree reserve, a community of more than 1,400 Indigenous people.

Other surprising results were the estimated 69% of adults satisfied with their spiritual life, 77% satisfied with their health, and 70% satisfied with their diet. Only 56% were satisfied with the quality of their sleep; 67% were satisfied with their work life; and only 56% were satisfied with their work-life balance.

With respect to belonging and trust, the Valleyview well-being survey showed that 62% of adult respondents had a strong or very strong sense of belonging to their neighborhood, while only 57% trusted most of their neighbors. Trust of businesses was high at 62% while very low for strangers: 25%. Over 74% of adults felt welcome and included in their neighborhood, yet only 53% felt safe walking alone at night through their town. Satisfaction with access to cultural events was low at only 29%, and only 37% of respondents felt satisfied with personal development opportunities.

In terms of the protection of the environment, only 56% felt their local municipal government was doing enough to protect the natural environment. Only 56% were satisfied with the local municipal government and town council.

While the citizens loved the quality of life a small town brings, they identified things that could be improved for enhancing their quality of life including: a) improving the aesthetic quality of the town's main street; b) more cultural, recreational and family-friendly activities; c) more variety of local shopping options; and d) more walking trails.

Citizens were also asked to rate or grade municipal government services and amenities. Grades as high as B+ to A were given to fire services, the local hospital, bylaw enforcement (policing) and water, sanitary and waste water treatment services. Lower grades (C and lower) were given to roads and sidewalks, early childhood prevention and planning and economic development.

The results have sparked an important conversation amongst all citizens in Valleyview. A natural question that arises is what to do with this information. Some may wonder, how does our community compare with others? Where should we focus our attention on improving the well-being conditions? Which citizens are doing more poorly in well-being than others? Is well-being unequally distributed in our community? Most importantly, the newly established Valleyview Well-Being Coalition has a mandate to improve the overall quality of life and well-being of their community, using the well-being assessment report to focus on those areas that citizens identified needing improvement. These included the aesthetics of Main Street and more sympathy extended to people in need, many of whom live on the street without a home or any personal connections.

The town council will also be using the well-being assessment results to establish strategic priorities and budgets for the coming fiscal year. The final step in this process is to formally incorporate the well-being assessment of community assets into the town's capital and operating budgets so that measuring the integrity of human, social and natural assets becomes as important as managing the long-term sustainability of the town's infrastructure. This is a step beyond what even Bhutan has thus far achieved.

Edmonton's Well-Being Index and Measuring the Well-Being Return on Taxes

Shortly after the publication of my first book, I received a call from the chief economist of the City of Edmonton, Paul Tsounis. Paul was interested in my work on the Alberta Genuine Progress Index and asked if I could create an exact replica of the 50-indicator well-being index. He explained that he felt such an index would be important for measuring Edmonton's progress against their new 10-year strategic plan, The Way Ahead. Furthermore, he envisioned the index being used to guide city budgeting.

The first Edmonton Well-Being Index was completed in 2008 and then updated in 2009. Figure 24 shows that the index peaked as early as 1982 (a year after the last major economic downturn) then fell steadily, reaching a low in 1997. Since then, the Edmonton Well-Being Index has shown steady improvements but had yet to reach the 1982 peak in 2008, the last year it was updated. At the same time, Edmonton's GDP has increased, with some interruptions due to economic downturns, especially the dramatic downturn of 2008 (during the major economic crisis).

I went a step further with the rich longitudinal data, running a statistical correlation analysis between Edmonton's GDP and the

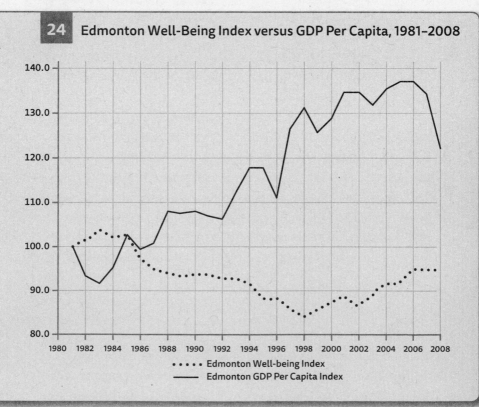

24 Edmonton Well-Being Index versus GDP Per Capita, 1981–2008

• • • • • Edmonton Well-being Index
——— Edmonton GDP Per Capita Index

SOURCE: Anielski Management Inc. 2009. The Edmonton 2008 Genuine Progress Indicator Report The State of Economic, Social and Environmental Wellbeing for the City of Edmonton.

other 49 economic, social, health and environmental well-being indicators over the 27-year period 1981–2008. This gave senior policy analysts and city council the ability to assess trends and attribute and even forecast the relationship between Edmonton's economic health and other key well-being indicators. This analysis produced some interesting results, including a strong statistical correlation between Edmonton's GDP growth and energy use, water quality index, household debt, personal consumption expenditures, ecological footprint, hazardous waste production, air quality index, domestic violence, life expectancy, weekly wage rate, educational attainment, obesity, youth drug use offences, and the value of public infrastructure.

Paul asked me to conduct five-year forecasts for future well-being for Edmonton based on these statistical correlations. While certainly not an exact science, the results suggested that changes in future well-being could be predicted with some degree of certainty, all things being equal, particularly during the next economic downturn or fall in oil prices. As noted earlier in reference to the Edmonton Social Health Index, Edmontonians seem to have remained relatively resilient in spite of rising and falling real GDP.

A key benefit to the Edmonton Well-Being Index was portraying 50 well-being indicators in the shape of a spider graphic or flower graphic (Figure 25). Portraying MS Excel data in this format has become my specialty. The benefit is that 50 well-being indicators for any given reporting year can be portrayed in a single image. A scale of 1 (worst condition) to 100 (best condition) is used to report on the well-being condition of each of the 50 well-being indicators; the resultant image clearly shows which conditions are flourishing and which are lagging. For example, the 2008 Edmonton Well-Being Index shows significant poor results for household debt, youth drug crime, problem gambling and Edmonton's carbon budget, as well as areas that are flourishing, including GDP, weekly wages, life expectancy, employment and water quality. The strength of this imagery is that it provides

25 Edmonton Well-Being Index, 2008

SOURCE: Anielski Management Inc. 2009. The Edmonton 2008 Genuine Progress Indicator Report The State of Economic, Social and Environmental Wellbeing for the City of Edmonton.

decision-makers with a quick visual tool for examining a number of well-being indicators and their interrelationships.

Another key benefit for Paul Tsounis was the correlation between the Edmonton Well-Being Index and property taxes. I suggested that this image would be the ultimate way of showing citizens the value of taxes relative to well-being conditions in the city. Figure 26 shows property taxes and user fees (in 2008 dollars) paid by Edmonton households relative to the Edmonton Well-Being Index. The image suggests a strong positive relationship between rising real per capita property taxes and the state of well-being in Edmonton.

While the Edmonton Well-Being Index has not been updated since 2009, the trends in the 22-indicator Edmonton Social Health Index show rising societal well-being relative to rising property taxes and user fee revenues (adjusted for inflation). Certainly the rate of change varies; real property taxes per capita increased 60% between 2000 and 2016, while Edmonton's Social Health Index

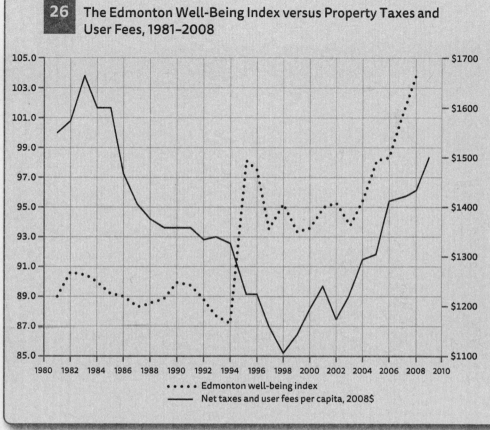

26 The Edmonton Well-Being Index versus Property Taxes and User Fees, 1981–2008

••••• Edmonton well-being index
——— Net taxes and user fees per capita, 2008$

SOURCE: Anielski Management Inc. 2009. The Edmonton 2008 Genuine Progress Indicator Report; The State of Economic, Social and Environmental Wellbeing for the City of Edmonton.

rose by 25% over the period 2000 to 2015. Notwithstanding, improved overall well-being is something to celebrate. While there is not necessarily a direct correlation between expenditure on municipal programs and services and an improved social health index, the image of an implied positive relationship is nevertheless compelling.

Community Asset and Well-Being-Impact-Based Governance

Today governments are experimenting with a number of new accountability systems, including outcome- and priority-based budgeting. Considerable progress has been made in the public sector toward linking budgets with the goals and even impacts of

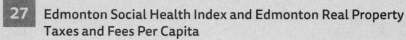

27 Edmonton Social Health Index and Edmonton Real Property Taxes and Fees Per Capita

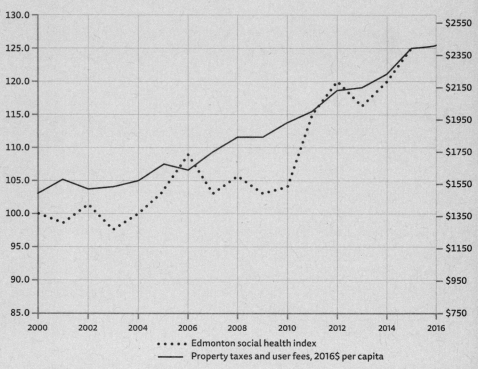

- - - - - Edmonton social health index
———— Property taxes and user fees, 2016$ per capita

SOURCE: City of Edmonton Annual Financials 2000–2016 and Edmonton Social Planning Council, Tracking the Trends 2015.

programs and services. The ultimate frontier is to demonstrate the well-being impacts of public sector programs and services. This requires an alignment of the overall mission, goals and strategies of programs to inputs, outputs, outcomes and well-being impacts. Well-being impacts are aligned with the five capital asset accounts of a community or organization, which are in turn linked to eight well-being domains and well-being indicators (both objective and subjective). The result is an integrated well-being decision-making and economic model for governing any community, municipality, province/state or nation. The same model can also be applied to corporations, whether for-profit or nonprofit, that adopt a well-being-benefit corporate structure.

For each of the five asset accounts and domains of well-being a series of well-being indicators are used to assess the current conditions and trends. For each domain of well-being, researchers ask

+ What are the current conditions of well-being?
+ What have been the short- and long-term trends in well-being?
+ How can the well-being conditions of this area of community well-being be improved?
+ What are the risks to future well-being if we do nothing?

The well-being accounting structure, broken down by five capital asset categories, well-being domains and well-being indicators (both objective and subjective), is shown in Table 6.

A comprehensive well-being audit is conducted using the well-being indicators above, statistics from conventional statistical data sources (e.g., Statistics Canada) and subjective well-being ratings from local well-being surveys conducted on a regular basis. The indicators currently show how poorly we understand what actually drives an economy or what makes an economy resilient.

The question of what makes any one asset class in the integrated five-asset model flourish requires an understanding of how each asset behaves, is impaired and can be strengthened. The assessment of the well-being condition of human, social and natural assets can be imagined as similar to your doctor evaluating your overall state of health using objective measures such as blood tests, blood pressure and reflex testing. In addition, your doctor may assess your mental and emotional state by asking subjective well-being questions of your current life. My doctor generally starts by asking me, "So, Mark, how is life? How is work? Are you getting enough exercise? Are you sleeping well? How is your relationship with your wife and kids?" They may even ask me about my spiritual well-being.

Just as my doctor will come up with an overall well-being assessment, so too can we apply the same assessment protocols to a

TABLE 6: Five Community Assets, Well-Being Domains, Indicators

Asset Category	Well-being Domain	Indicators
Human Assets	Work	Employment and unemployment rate, labor force participation, occupation diversity index, average work week (hours), unpaid work (volunteerism), perceptions of meaningful work and workplace environment.
	Time Use	Paid work, volunteerism, time with family, children, parents, elders, leisure time.
	Health	Happiness and life satisfaction perceptions, life expectancy, disease rates (cancer, diabetes, high blood pressure), smoking, drinking, self-rated health.
	Physical Well-Being	Body-Mass Index, perceptions of physical health, diet and quality of sleep.
	Psychological Well-Being	Mental and emotional self-ratings, hope index, enjoyment of life index, life stress index, suicide rates.
	Spiritual Well-Being	Perceived spiritual well-being.
	Family Cohesion	Domestic violence, trust and belonging.
	Learning/ Education	Educational attainment, perceptions of access to education and skill development.
Social Assets	Ethnic Diversity and Inclusion	Diversity of ethnic and language groups, feelings of inclusion.
	Trust and Belonging	Perceptions of trust and belonging.
	Safety and Crime	Crime rates, perceptions of personal safety.
	Equity and Fairness	Distribution of income and wealth, women and minorities representation.
	Democratic Engagement	Voter participation, satisfaction with governance.
Natural Assets	Ecological Footprint	Material, energy and carbon footprint per household, WalkScore (walkability index), population density.
	Sustainable Food Production	Local sustainable food production, agricultural soil productivity.

TABLE 6 (cont'd.): Five Community Assets, Well-Being Domains, Indicators

Asset Category	Well-being Domain	Indicators
	Environmental Integrity, Ecosystem Health	Ecosystem integrity and resilience index, ecosystem service values, air quality index, water quality index, pollution release index, unfunded environmental liabilities (e.g., toxic soils, brownfields).
	Energy, Water and Waste	Energy reserve life (oil, gas, coal and renewables), renewable energy capacity, energy end use, energy efficiency, water use, water footprint, waste to landfills, toxic waste, recycling rates.
	Natural Resources	Land area, productivity and values for watersheds, forests, wetlands, agricultural land, energy and minerals reserve life, timber sustainability index.
Built Assets	Housing	Housing stock, housing starts, age of housing stock, maintenance liabilities, cost of housing/rent.
	Public Infrastructure	Roads, sidewalks, walking/bike trails, sewers, pipe, buildings, recreation facilities, parks, playgrounds, hospitals; satisfaction with and ratings of public amenities and infrastructure.
	Intangible Assets	Patents, trademarks, copyrights, ideas, artistic assets, contracts, databases and software.
Financial/ Economic Assets	Economic Vitality	GDP, businesses, business diversity index, small business vitality, economic diversity index, citizen perceptions of economic vitality.
	Living Standards	Household income, lone-parent families, households living below poverty line, living wages, work hours required to generate living wage, food bank use, happiness rating per $1000 of household income.
	Financial Security	Incidence of low-income households, perceptions of financial sufficiency and financial stress.
	Affordable Housing	Ratio of housing prices to household income, average housing prices, rental rates, percentage of households in need of affordable housing.
	Affordable and Efficient Government	Municipal government expenditures, property tax revenues, ratings of municipal programs, services and infrastructure/amenities.

community, workplace, corporation or nation by using both objective and subjective indicators to evaluate the current state of well-being and trends over time.

Well-Being-Based Governance and Budgeting

Using well-being as a measure to guide behavior and decision-making will require more than simply the desire to improve well-being. Well-being-outcome-based budgeting can become part of the aspirational consciousness of city councils, parliaments and legislatures worldwide.

There is no easy or efficient path toward the goal of well-being-based decision-making whether in the public or private or non-profit sectors. The journey will be one of experimentation and continuous improvement. Figure 28 provides a conceptual model

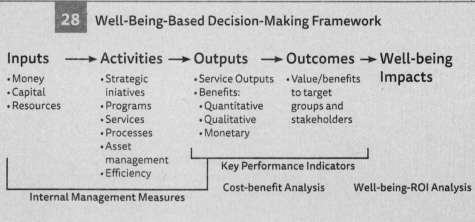

28   Well-Being-Based Decision-Making Framework

Inputs →	Activities →	Outputs →	Outcomes →	Well-being Impacts
• Money • Capital • Resources	• Strategic iniatives • Programs • Services • Processes • Asset management • Efficiency	• Service Outputs • Benefits: • Quantitative • Qualitative • Monetary	• Value/benefits to target groups and stakeholders	

Internal Management Measures

Key Performance Indicators

Cost-benefit Analysis   Well-being-ROI Analysis

Resources dedicated to or consumed by the program or service (e.g., money, staff, volunteers, facilities, equipment, supplies).	What is done with the inputs to deliver its purpose/mission in terms of the needs of target group or stakeholder needs (e.g., food and shelter, job skills, educate, and counsel).	The direct products of the program or service activities (e.g., number of classes taught, number of participants, sessions, and volume of materials distributed).	The results, value or benefits to target groups and stakeholders needs resulting from program service delivery.	Impacts/benefits to well-being on beneficiaries and various stakeholders of policies, programs, and services.

SOURCE: Anielski Management Inc. 2016.

for well-being-based decision-making, which will be familiar to many in the public sector, however, with well-being impacts as the ultimate aspiration.

The fundamental question to be answered from a well-being-based governance model is

What is the expected impact (positive, neutral or negative) of the policy or budgetary decision we are making today?

Tying decision-making to these well-being indicators or accounts keeps the decision-making process focused on current conditions and trends in well-being, with the goal of improving well-being conditions, where needed.

If decision-makers were enabled to answer the well-being value for taxes question, then citizens would be well served to understand the value of programs and services of the public sector.

A well-being-based budgeting system would help to demonstrate the well-being impacts or outcomes associated with program and service capital and operating budgets. Budgets represent future effort measured in terms of money and resources that are dedicated to maintaining the benefits of programs, services and assets or amenities under the management of community, city, state and national governments, and even corporations.

While traditional capital asset budgeting has focused on tangible assets such as roads, pipes and conventional infrastructure, these new means of measuring intangible assets using well-being proxies make accounting and budgeting for human, social and natural assets possible. Determining how a conventional asset such as a building or a road contributes to the well-being of a neighborhood would represent a seismic shift in value accounting and reporting. In other words, a well-being-return-on asset accounting future is within our grasp.

This expansion of traditional asset accounting methods will require a new generation of management accountants, chief economists, CFOs, auditors and city managers who will generate well-being impact and benefit reports for city councils and for annual reports to citizens. The strategic question to be contemplated will be How will our capital, operating and programs/service budgets affect the five assets and well-being domains for our city? How can we improve well-being conditions across all neighborhoods in a city?

Designing a New Economy of Well-Being for Tahiti (French Polynesia)

Advancing the new economic model based on well-being has not been without its challenges. Certainly the most exotic of my recent experiences was presenting my ideas for building a new economy of well-being to the South Pacific paradise of French Polynesia. I was invited in July 2012 to Tahiti to present my vision for a new economy of well-being (*économie du bonheur*) at a youth forum called Build Me a Nation, hosted by the president of French Polynesia, Oscar Temaru, and the senator to France, Richard Tuheiva. Former French Polynesian Tourism Minister Marc Collins had been trying to bring me to Tahiti to advise Temaru's caucus for the preceding two years. This was my chance to present my model to the president and other senior members of his government and key opposition members.

I made my first presentation to an audience of young persons, diplomats from other South Pacific nations, the French Polynesian President Oscar Temaru, Senator Richard Tuheiva and others at the Build Me a Nation conference. The youth were very inspired by what I proposed, as was President Temaru. He was so intrigued with my proposed economic well-being and sovereign asset model that he invited me to provide a full briefing in his office along with the vice president and finance minister.

I outlined a strategy by which a comprehensive asset inventory would be conducted for all of the islands and seascape of this 5,000-square-kilometer region of the South Pacific (an area larger than Europe) with nearly 300,000 people. I described to his finance minister how a national strategic asset management plan would be developed along with budgets that would be directly tied to a balance sheet for the nation. After a two-hour meeting, followed by a French Polynesian cuisine dinner in the presidential dining room, I was asked to prepare a formal proposal for the president and his caucus.

While compelled by the economic model, President Temaru felt that it might be politically risky to propose it for all of French Polynesia without first pilot testing it in his own community of Faa'a; Temaru had been mayor of Faa'a, one of the poorest communities in Tahiti, for more than 25 years and was respected there.

The strategy was to test the economic model, including a comprehensive well-being assessment, creation of a well-being index and implementation of a well-being-based asset planning, budgeting and governance system for at least one city in French Polynesia. The proposed model was identical to what had just been accomplished with the town of Valleyview in Alberta.

Oscar Temaru was unable to win political support for the Faa'a project from other members of his Faa'a community. Moreover, he lost the 2013 national election, having campaigned on a platform of decolonization from France.

At the same time Temaru was unable to secure political support in his community, Senator Richard Tuheiva, who lived in the Commune of Arue on Tahiti, was able to obtain a grant from French funders to create a new association, Te'Oaoa Ia Hotu (May Joy Flourish), whose mission was to assess the well-being of the 9,000 people of Arue and develop a well-being index.

In November 2017, five years after my first visit, I journeyed to Tahiti to conduct a community well-being assessment using a well-being survey, in both French and Tahitian. Richard, his wife Karine, Parii Aroita (president of the association) and his wife Jolina formed the core team in the development of the Arue Well-Being and Happiness Index. The survey was modeled, in part, after the Canadian Index of Wellbeing and Bhutan's Gross National Happiness, to assess a number of perceptional aspects of well-being. These included overall self-rating of well-being; life satisfaction; hope for the future; mental, emotional, and physical health; quality of sleep; spiritual well-being; rating of the local economy; financial and material well-being; work-life balance; relationships and trust of others (including politicians);

and perceptions of the natural environment. Our team met with groups of local citizens, leaders from the Protestant, Catholic and Mormon churches, and the media.

At one evening event, an elderly man remarked on how unique this project was. He noted that people are rarely asked about how they actually feel about their lives. That same evening the Tahitians agreed to dedicate the well-being index work to a famous Tahitian motto coined by a legendary poet and elder: *Te aroha ia rahi* ("May our love flourish"). The Tahitian word *aroha* has the same meaning as the Hawaiian word *aloha*: "love."

Over the two-week survey period I witnessed a remarkable shift in consciousness and gained a renewed appreciation of Tahitian and Polynesian culture. The Tahitians thanked me for renewing their eight core values, which are

+ *aroha* (unconditional love, compassion)
+ *parau* (orality and languages)
+ *varua* (spirituality and faith)
+ *natura* (natural ecosystems, including *moana* [ocean], *fenua* [land] and *reva* [sky])
+ *nunaa* (community)
+ *peu* (customs and traditions)
+ *mana* (leadership, responsibilities, governance)
+ *tau* (seasons, time)

The Arue Well-Being Index would henceforth be aligned with these eight core Tahitian values. Preliminary results of the survey revealed some interesting trends, including high levels of self-rated and spiritual well-being yet lower-than-expected levels of life satisfaction and financial well-being. Like similar well-being measurement projects, the results are already beginning to generate an important conversation in the community and is now spreading to other parts of Tahiti and French Polynesia. The survey has sparked a conversation about what it means to be Tahitian and Polynesian in a country that remains a colony of France. The hope is that this conversation and the use of the index will spread across other Polynesian communities and nations from New Zealand to Hawai'i.

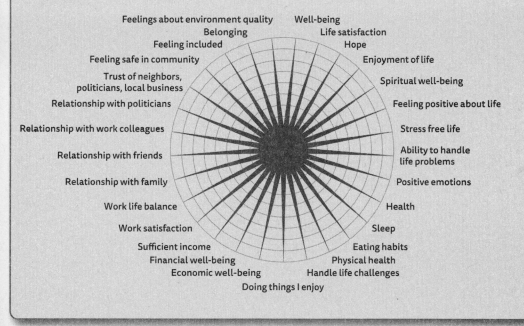

29 The Arue (Tahiti) Well-Being Index

SOURCE: Mark Anielski and the Association of Te OaOa Hotu.

Richard Tuheiva, who represents a new generation of young political leaders, envisions the Arue project inspiring similar well-being measurement initiatives throughout French Polynesia and Oceania, leading to a new economic model based focused less on money and material growth (as measured by GDP) and more on improving well-being, in ways rooted in traditional Tahitian values.

It seems fitting that Tahiti would become a model of a new économie *du bonheur* (economy of happiness), given the Polynesians' long history of navigating the vast South Pacific Ocean using the Moon and the stars and adopting seashells as the world's oldest form of money.

Notes

1. The Edmonton Social Planning Council is an independent, nonprofit, charitable organization that focuses on social research, particularly in the areas of low income and poverty.

CHAPTER 5

Well-Being for First Nations

WORKING WITH FIRST NATIONS, Métis and Inuit people in Canada has been a rewarding experience. These Indigenous people of Canada have a great deal to contribute to the economic paradigm of well-being.

First Nations see the world in the form of relationships, circles, wheels or hoops, not linear GDP growth lines. Most do not understand the Western mind of money and material wealth accumulation. Most see nature as the model of the economy; nature is viewed as being abundant and life-giving. Nature does not hoard, nor does the Creator (God) give without expectation of a financial return. This suggests they see the world as integral whole, a circle of life, and a union and harmony of diverse parts—the notion of all-my-relations. Indigenous people are likely to subscribe to the circular economy model that sees waste and food and money as a flow, not something to be stored up or hoarded. This world view suggests an economy of harmony and balance, founded on grace and trust.

As an economist accustomed to images of upward sloping demand curves, rising GDP, income, and inflation, spending time with First Nations and Inuit people over the past 15 years has revealed new images of an economy of interrelationships in a circle of well-being indicators.

The image of a spider's web or flower petals comes to mind. The Fibonacci sequence or golden mean observed in nature. The Fibonacci is a series of numbers that follow an integer sequence of progression. Fibonacci numbers appear unexpectedly often in

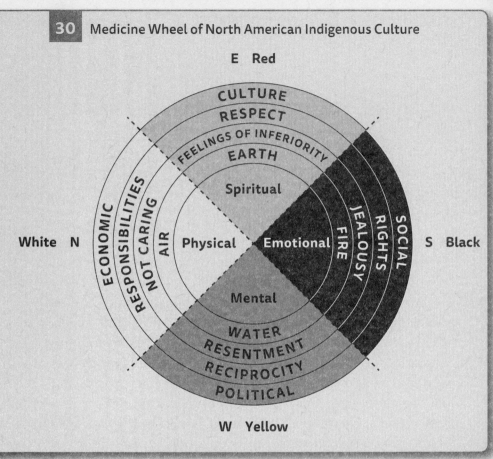

30 Medicine Wheel of North American Indigenous Culture

SOURCE: trauma-informed.ca/trauma-and-first-nations-people/cultural-practices/the-medicine-wheel/.

mathematics and also in nature, such as in the sequence of petals and seeds in a sunflower, the branching in trees, the arrangement of leaves on a stem, the fruit sprouts of a pineapple, an uncurling fern and the arrangement of a pine cone's bracts.

First Nations, Métis and Inuit people in Canada live according to the wisdom of the medicine wheel, or hoop of life, though there are various interpretations of the term used to represent the sacred wheel. The "medicine wheel" is not a native term but was used by early American settlers to describe the large rock circles found near Sheridan, Wyoming, and elsewhere across the Great Plains.[1]

There are a number of interpretations of the medicine wheel

used by different First Nations peoples and cultures. The medicine wheel teachings are based on a circular pattern and cyclical set of four: the four seasons, the four stages of life, a person's four biopsychosocial and spiritual aspects. The medicine wheel always centers on the individual, representing a human person with four aspects: mental (north), spiritual (east), physical (west) and emotional (south) attributes. These four attributes and four directions are in harmony with each other as represented by the circle and the lines that unit the four aspects. The wheel turns smoothly and clockwise like a well-balanced wheel through time (a lifetime), driven by volition or free will, which exists in the central axis of the wheel. The center represents harmony and balance, perhaps the heart and soul of each human being. Some believe the sun is what shines through the center of each person's soul. Each person has his or own unique aspects, gifts, skills, dreams and aspirations. When integrated together in households and communities, we have the intersection of multiple medicine wheels forming a web of interrelationship, which in turn is in harmony with Nature, or Mother Earth.

Indigenous peoples of North America (known to them as Turtle Island) have lived with this mindset and model for an economy for more than ten thousand years in a life of harmonious relationship with nature. This complex relationship with Mother Earth does not require gold or paper currency or merchant banks. It is defined by mutual exchange of material things, including food, clothing and things of adornment or jewelry. The only form of currency for exchange was at one time seashells: the kauri and dentalium shells. The former originated in the South Pacific where the Maori and Polynesian peoples lived, the latter from the west coast of Turtle Island. The use of shells as money dates back to ancient island of Taiwan and Chinese cultures predating the use of coins. Why seashells? Perhaps they reflect the higher value and rarity of things such as obsidian, which was rare in the prairie ecosystem.

Lewis Cardinal, a member of the Sucker Creek Cree First Nation in Northern Alberta, has taught me the story of Edmonton, my home, as the great gathering place, or *pehonen*, of Turtle Island. For more than ten thousand years people from many nations gathered at what author Jared Diamond (*Guns, Germs and Steel*, 1997) called the edge of the great continental ice sheet, "the happy hunting grounds." Few Edmontonians today have ever heard this story.

Edmonton is situated at the bottom of an ancient glacial lake. The Elders who taught Lewis about the story of Edmonton reminded him the city's name contains the word *Monto*, which in Cree means "Great Spirit." The reason so many nations from all four directions gathered in Edmonton was to trade in stories, materials and families. A complex system of interrelationships was established in which differences were set aside and mutual cooperation meant that every group of peoples or Nations could survive and flourish across the various ecosystems and landscapes.

This highly functional and resilient economic system lasted for thousands of years until the European settlers came in the 1850s, first as missionaries and pioneers. The Western economic system eventually led to the downfall of the economic customs of these Indigenous peoples. Elaborate systems of exchange, including the potlatch, were signs of the truth of the abundance of Mother Earth and their reliance on her abundant gifts. Ceremonies like the sweat lodge were used as a form of their spiritual connectedness to the Earth and to be reminded that we are all alone and sometimes in darkness.

The wampum belt formed from seashells sewn onto strips of deer hide or moose hide became the dominant form of treaties and some believe were a form of currency for exchange. Wampum beads were used to create intricate patterns on belts that were used as a guide to narrate Haudenosaunee or Iroquois history, traditions and laws. Historians have proved that wampum may have been the first form of currency used by the early American colonists. For the Haudenosaunee people, wampum was sacred. Wampum served as a person's credentials or a certificate of authority. Wampum was also used for official purposes and religious ceremonies.

In late January 2014, I had the honor of being invited to meet the Onondaga Nation on their traditional lands located on their sacred Lake Onondaga near Syracuse, New York. I was there with a group of environmental scientists, economists and Indigenous Elders called the Seven Eagles to offer our strategic services to the Onondaga people to help find solutions to the environmental degradation of their traditional lands. Their sacred Lake Onondaga, considered of great spiritual and cultural importance to the Iroquois, had suffered from 100 years' contamination from mercury and other chemicals leaching into Lake Onondaga from Allied Chemicals and Honeywell. The US Environmental Protection Agency has declared the lake a Superfund site, one of the most polluted lakes in the United States, and ordered its cleanup.

It was on these shores of Lake Onondaga that the Iroquois, or Haudenosaunee, were given their Great Law of Peace by a visitor they claim came from a far over 2,000 years ago. It has been part of their culture and governance structure ever since. The Great

31 Onondaga Nation Sacred Tree and 50-Clans Image, Onondaga Nation, New York

SOURCE: Photo by Mark Anielski, Onondaga Nation, March 2014.

Law is defined by a Tree of Peace and a Circle (Figure 31). The Great Tree of Peace is a symbol of peace: all the Chiefs stand around it in a circle, arms linked, to support it and prevent it from falling over. Atop the tree sits an eagle to see far and wide and warn of danger.

After a five-hour drive from New York City we entered the traditional longhouse of the Onondaga, one of the "Six Nations" of the Haudenosaunee, or Iroquois. We were greeted by the clan mothers, Grand Chief Sid Hill and 83-year-old Oren Lyons, the faith keeper of the Turtle Clan of the Onondaga Nation of the Haudenosaunee (Iroquois) Confederacy. The Haudenosaunee have a matrilineal kinship system of governance, with descent and inheritance passing through maternal lines. The clan mothers, the Elder women of each clan, are highly respected; they have the power to elect or remove a chief that represents their clan. The women Elders nominate the chief for life from the clan and own the symbols of his office. While men serve as chiefs, the real power resides with the clan mothers, the keepers of the sacred laws of the water and the land.

We entered the longhouse that chilly afternoon in January to a stunning sight that still amazes me. The clan mothers were seated on the extended side of the longhouse. On the walls were the osprey-feathered headdresses of the 50 clan chiefs. In the middle of the room, laid out on a long table, was the 1794 Canadaigua Treaty wampum belt that George Washington had commissioned to ratify a treaty between the US colonies and the Haudenosaunee to end quarrels between them. Wampum belts are spiritually and culturally revered as living treaties still binding today. This belt treaty defined the peaceful coexistence of each nation, going back to the Two-Row Wampum agreed by the Dutch and Haudenosaunee in 1613, in which the two parties agreed to respect each other's laws and customs and not interfere in the internal affairs of the other. For the Onondaga Nation, the Two-Row Wampum Treaty remains the basis of the aspiration of peaceful coexistence between the citizens of New York state and the Haudenosaunee residents of the Onondaga Lake region. According to Oren Lyons, the treaty states that

32 The Circle Wampum

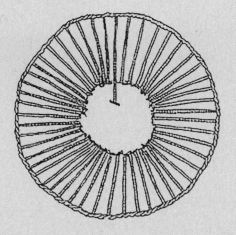

SOURCE: Onondaga Nation. onondaganation.org/culture/wampum/circle-wampum/. Accessed May 30, 2017.

As long as the Sun shines upon this Earth, that is how long our Agreement will stand; Second, as long as the Water still flows; and Third, as long as the Grass Grows Green at a certain time of the year. Now we have Symbolized this Agreement and it shall be binding forever as long as Mother Earth is still in motion.[2]

I sat across the table from Onondaga Faithkeeper Oren Lyons and Grand Chief Sid Hill. Lyons, the 83-year-old chief and spirit keeper of the Turtle Clan, shared with us his knowledge of money and his understanding of how the book and movie *The Wizard of Oz* connected to First Nations people. He explained that the flying monkeys in *The Wizard of Oz* represented Indians and the Wicked Witch of the West represented Mother Nature.[3] He explained that it was Abraham Lincoln's *Homestead Act* that resulted in a flood of American settlers to the western states, thus destroying the Indigenous cultures, their way of life and Mother Nature.

Oren Lyons painted a picture of a new future for both First Nations and others based on a circle wampum belt. The circle wampum (Figure 32) is a very important belt for the Haudenosaunee. The equal strands of wampum represent the 50 chiefs of the

Onondaga Nation, each chief being equal and all being united. The single longer strand represents the people. When we are born, our heart is in the middle of the circle. As we grow, the chiefs and the people work to keep the circle in harmony. The image reminded me of the circular graphs I had been using to represent well-being, an image of harmony, balance and unity. But it differs from the images our minds have been accustomed to: pyramidal hierarchies such as the Great Seal on the US one-dollar bill and Maslow's hierarchy of needs.

Oren and I discussed the future of money and the future of the United States. He saw great strife and conflict arising across the land, over natural resources and water. He saw financial turmoil causing a flight of economic refugees from New York and the large cities. I couldn't help think about the shortsightedness of the United States' colonists who founded their colonies on the Iroquois Confederacy model but otherwise failed to embrace the Indigenous wisdom of harmony with nature, a model for an economy well-being. The United States, after winning the Revolutionary War with Britain over monetary sovereignty, has become the most indebted and debt-enslaved nation on earth. How sad that the beautiful Indigenous culture that had been gifted the Great Law of Peace—the oral constitution of the Haudensosaunee Nation—more than two thousand years ago by a mysterious visitor (the Great Peacemaker) on the very shores of Lake Onondaga would now struggle to reclaim the integrity of their sacred lake. They might still remind current presidents and Congress of the wisdom of their Elders and clan mothers.[4]

According to Carol Anne Hilton—a member of the Nuu-chah-nulth Nation on Vancouver Island and the CEO of Transformation, a First Nation socioeconomic consulting firm—First Nations are defining their modern presence and need to delineate their future through participation in the Canadian economy. She has coined a new economic paradigm *indigenomics*. Indigenomics acts as a vehicle for understanding, creating meaning and expressing her people's Indigenous relationship to economies. With the recent

Canada Supreme Court decision in favor of the Tsilhqot'in Nation, and numerous other court rulings such as the Nuu-chah-nulth case, the definition of wealth within the economic system of this country through the First Nation relationship is emerging. The question all of us, both Indigenous and non-Indigenous, need to answer is, "What new thinking is now required of us?"

Carol-Anne Hilton believes the time is now to build a collective toolbox to fill with our deepest questions—to find out why, how, and what is possible in the search for deeper meaning and relevance to new economies: economies of well-being. There is a shift in measuring progress in terms of measuring well-being impacts. People are simply expecting more of our economies that aligns with their aspirations for improved well-being and quality of life.

Measuring What Matters to Community Well-Being

First Nation, Métis and Inuit communities understand the value of family, traditions, culture, and Mother Nature. To secure a resilient economic future and be business and investment ready, communities also need to understand the potential economic well-being benefits of their community assets. These include human (people), social (relationships, trust), cultural (traditions), built (infrastructure), natural (land, resources, water, traditional use) and economic assets. Good decision-making requires an assessment of the potential of a community's assets within a planning framework that encompasses technical, business, legal, political, social and spiritual strategies for improved well-being.

My hope is to work with First Nation, Métis and Inuit communities and businesses to provide them with strategic economic advice to help build the capacity to achieve economic self-sufficiency and a flourishing culture of well-being. Most Indigenous communities, while materially and financial impoverished, are genuinely wealthy in tiers of culture, traditions, people, land, and natural resources that reside both on their reserve lands and with their traditional territory. I see First Nations as the early adopters of a new economic paradigm of well-being.

Why a Community Asset Assessment?

The first step in First Nations controlling their own destiny (economic self-sufficiency) is determining the current potential of a community's assets and envisioning what the future could look like. This begins with engaging the community in an assessment of the community's assets, using an integrated five-capital community asset assessment process.

Taking a well-being-based approach to community planning, development, governance and accountability will redefine the way First Nations participate in the Canadian economy. A well-being-based community asset development and investment approach to local governance will strengthen the perception of First Nations investment and business development opportunities in the eyes of Canada's financial institutions. Taking a well-being return on investment approach to assessing First Nations community asset development will set a new precedent in Canada's financial services sector.

Natural Capital Assessment

Natural capital including land, water, animals, plants, herbs and traditional medicines are of critical value to First Nations and their ability to flourish on the land. The 2014 Supreme Court of Canada ruling in favor of the Tsilhqot'in First Nation in northeastern British Columbia (Williams Lake area) clarified that First Nations have the right to enjoy the benefits of land and resources, which include traditional hunting, fishing and land use, that lie within their traditional territory. The unanimous 8–0 Supreme Court decision resolves many important legal questions, such as how to determine Aboriginal title and whether provincial laws apply to those lands.[5] The decision has implications for future economic or resource development on First Nations lands that have been unresolved for over 150 years since the first treaties were signed in the 1860s.

This raises other fundamental issues with respect to the legal rights of Mother Nature itself. In March 2017, the Maori people of

Aotearoa (the Māori name for New Zealand) succeeded in pass-ing the Te Awa Tupua (Whanganui River Claims Settlement).[6] The Whanganui River is the largest navigable river in Aotearoa. The new bill means it has become the first watershed in the world to be recognized as a rights-bearing entity, holding the legal status "personhood." This means that the river and its natural assets and ecosystem functions are no longer the property of the Crown/New Zealand government. In essence, Mother Nature owns itself. This has profound implications for similar aspirations of First Nations in Canada and around the world, who have long believed that no one has property rights or ownership over Mother Nature, be it land, water or sky.

For First Nations like the Maori, the Tahitians and the Hawai-ians, formalizing the legal recognition of the rights of ecosystems simply affirms their long-held cultural and spiritual beliefs that "I am the river. I am the ocean. I am the tree. I am the universe. The river, the ocean and the tree is me." According to their beliefs and values, there is no separation between humans and nature; the mountains and rivers are their ancestors. They consider these natural forces to be spiritual living beings. Therefore, to cause harm to Mother Nature through resource extraction or pollution is to literally injure one's own body and community. This major seismic shift in property rights in consistent with the Natural Laws of Indigenous peoples around the world.

If Canada's First Nations can secure similar legal rights for Mother Nature, recognizing the personhood of a river, a forest or a wetland within their traditional territories like the Maori have done, thus taking ownership away from the Crown (the govern-ment of Canada and ultimately the Queen/Westminster), this will be the first step in ensuring that nature itself can begin to heal from the damage we have inflicted on it through our own prop-erty rights hubris.

The New Zealand precedent means that nobody owns the land—rather, the land owns itself. This then shifts land and re-source management one step toward sovereignty for Indigenous peoples, whose identity is inseparable from the land. As Kara

Puketapu Dentice, the grandson of the great Maori chief Kara Puketapu (Waiwhetu) and a land use planner and manager for the Maori Whanganui River Settlement, reminded me in November 2017 (during a TEDx Talk in Arue, Tahiti), our responsibility is to be in *pono* (right relationship) with Mother Earth. This can be accomplished only by recognizing that the mountains, forests and watersheds can be better protected by making sure that human responsibilities to the whole ecosystem take priority over resource extraction licenses. From now on, stewardship decisions about development in the Whanganui River watershed will be made by a council of two appointees—one Crown and one Māori—who will act on behalf of the river to uphold and protect its values, health and well-being.

This remarkable seismic shift gives us hope that land and water stewardship in Canada between First Nations and the Crown can become more harmonious, ensuring long-term well-being benefits to human populations while guaranteeing flourishing ecosystems. This would also represent an important step toward securing future economic well-being for First Nations, who may at last be able to speak for the well-being interests of current and future generations, not just of people but also of the forests, rivers, oceans and sky, as their spiritual relatives. I see this future as a win-win-win scenario for First Nations, provincial governments and industry, if the goal is to ensure the highest and best well-being returns on investment of time and energy in the wise stewardship of land, water and natural resources.

A natural capital assessment of the broadest suite of Mother Nature's natural assets and unpriced ecosystem services that is aligned with the Natural Laws and these new legal structures will become the basis for sustainable land, water and air stewardship in Canada and around the world.

The Well-Being Community Planning Process

The community asset assessment and well-being planning process for First Nations begins by engaging the entire community in a dialogue about their values, needs, hopes, aspirations, Indigenous laws and traditions. The result is shared community's values and a mutual understanding of the needs, gifts, skills, competencies and dreams of all members and clans of the Nations for a better life. It will also effect the articulation of Indigenous laws—most of which have been oral and never codified. Once codified, these Indigenous laws will form the basis of the governance of Indigenous economies of well-being that will in turn be respected by traditional courts of law in Canada.

An inventory and assessment of the community's five assets of well-being will be conducted similar to the assessment for Valleyview, Alberta. The conditions of well-being can be assessed using surveys, but in First Nations communities, dialogue or sharing circles are likely to be more meaningful to their culture. Community well-being conditions will be assessed at the individual, household and clan levels, including assessing the mental, physical, emotional and spiritual aspects of the medicine wheel, along with other well-being metrics used in Bhutan or the Town of Valleyview.

A proper accounting and valuation of a First Nation's wealth or assets will ensure it is investment-ready to establish key partnerships for impact investors, businesses and economic development. The community asset assessment be conducted in consultation with the chief and council, clans (clan mothers), Elders, programs and services, members and other stakeholders. Through these deliberations, a First Nation community will develop a community asset well-being development plan and strategy for economic, employment and business development

Accounting for the comprehensive wealth of a First Nation, using fair market and non-market valuations of the Nation's assets, will strengthen that Nation's capacity to negotiate agreements with government and industry that are in the best interests of all peoples as well as Mother Nature. To control a First Nation's destiny means to command the proper valuation of the Nation's assets in a manner that will be honored as legitimate by federal and provincial governments, accounting firms, banks and investors but also valued in traditional ways that Elders will respect.

Preparing a community well-being strategic plan and budgets will empower the Nation to better identify and manage the potential benefits of your assets for seven and more generations.

Similar to the Maori in New Zealand, a few First Nations in Alberta have begun to conduct well-being and community asset assessments on their path to economic self-determination. This is an important step for First Nations, Métis and Inuit people in Canada to pursue the same quality of life that other Canadians currently enjoy.

Benefits of a Well-Being-Based Approach to Community Development

The benefit of a well-being-based approach to community development is that it makes community well-being the ultimate goal of economic development.

According to Carol Anne Hilton, there are three essential elements of these new Indigenous economies:

+ Strengthened relationships;
+ Deeper purpose and relevance to the future, and;
+ A collaborative shift in measurement of new economies.

By measuring the true potential of its people, lands, resources and culture, a First Nation is better equipped to become a model of the new economy of well-being. These communities will become role models and centers of excellence for hundreds of other communities in governance, education, employment, training, health, community development and, ultimately, well-being.

The community of individuals, households, clans and businesses will be better informed about their real wealth or well-being, the potential for developing the full potential of human, social-cultural, natural and built (infrastructure) assets for long-lasting well-being benefits. This will lead to better and wiser community well-being planning and development of the community assets in such a way that makes the best of individual and collective skills, talents, competencies and aspirations. Chief and council will be better informed to make decisions that are oriented toward making the highest and best use of the community's shared assets and make well-being returns on investments (well-being ROI), the new bottom line for accountability to the people of the Nation, attracting a new generation of impact investors who want to contribute to a more hopeful future.

The overall community will be informed about the state and potential of their community's well-being renewing their traditions and Indigenous laws. This builds capacity for greater economic independency and less reliance on federal and provincial government funding.

Notes

1. Source: dancingtoeaglespiritsociety.org/medwheel.php. Accessed June 1, 2017.
2. Personal conversation with Oren Lyons, January 25, 2014, in the Onondaga Nation near Lake Onondaga.
3. See Oren Lyons speaking about Native American people and The Wizard of Oz at youtu.be/t8ttzSwYFa8. Accessed June 1, 2017.
4. According to Haudensosaunee traditions, the law was written on wampum belts conceived by Dekanawidah, The Great Peacemaker, and his spokesman Hiawatha. The original five member nations ratified this constitution near modern-day Victor, New York, with the sixth nation (the Tuscarora) being added in c. 1722. The laws were first recorded and transmitted not in written language but by means of wampum symbols that conveyed meaning. In a later era these were translated into English and now survive in various accounts. The Great Law of Peace is presented as part of a narrative noting laws and ceremonies to be performed at prescribed times. The laws, called a constitution, are divided into 117 articles.
5. The interpretation of Canada's top court remains open to debate and testing of resource title boundaries. Canada's top court agreed that a seminomadic tribe can claim land title even if it uses it only some of the time, and it set out a three-point test to determine land titles, considering a) occupation, b) continuity of habitation on the land, and c) exclusivity in area. The court also established what title means, including the right to the benefits associated with the land and the right to use it, enjoy it and profit from it. However, the court declared that title is not absolute, meaning economic development can still proceed on land where title is established as long as one of two conditions is met: a) the development has the consent of the First Nation, and b) failing that, the government must make the case that development is pressing and substantial and meets its fiduciary duty to the aboriginal group.
6. earthisland.org/journal/index.php/elist/eListRead/when_rivers _hold_legal_rights/. Accessed December 8, 2017.

CHAPTER 6

The Well-Being
Workplace

WHAT IF THE ULTIMATE GOAL and purpose of business was to contribute to the overall well-being of society and to create conditions for the highest possible workplace well-being? Instead of the adage of profit maximization and shareholder primacy, imagine business leaders adopting the late Ray Anderson's corporate motto of "Doing well by doing good."[1]

Augmenting financial performance, customer satisfaction, and other productivity measures with well-being metrics of workplace well-being would provide a more balanced profile of corporate performance. The emergence of the Benefit Corporation (B-Corp)—the purpose of a benefit corporation is to create general public benefit, which is defined as a material positive impact on society and the environment—is a positive trend toward a new business that considers more than simply profit maximization to include the company's social and environmental performance. This is an important progression to what I believe will be the ultimate corporate structure: the well-being corporation.

A well-being enterprise or corporation would define its corporate mandate and "best interests" in terms of workplace, community, and environmental well-being as its highest aspiration. The well-being corporation would be governed based on a common set of criteria for well-being, based on the science and determinants of well-being. I believe that in the future the legal documents (the corporate charter) that give rise to corporations will define their best interest in terms of well-being of employees, the community and the environment. This will require new accounting and reporting systems to satisfy a new generation of leaders and boards of directors who will want evidence of the positive impacts the corporation is having on relationships, trust, customer satisfaction, and workplace well-being. Ultimately these well-being corporations will be able to demonstrate higher rates of well-being return on investments in the assets under management for both internal and external accountability. While financial performance indicators will remain important for assessing the vitality of an enterprise, they will be complemented by a broader suite of well-being impact indicators.

Well-Being at Work

According to Gallup, the majority of American and Canadian workers experience very little meaning in their day-to-day work. According to Gallup's 2011–12 global study (142 countries surveyed) of workplace well-being, only 13% of employees worldwide feel engaged at work. The State of the Global Workplace study found that only one in eight workers (13%)—roughly 180 million employees in the countries studied—are psychologically committed to their jobs and likely to be making positive contributions to their organizations. The bulk of employees worldwide—63%—are "not engaged," meaning they lack motivation and are less likely to invest discretionary effort in organizational goals or outcomes. And 24% are "actively disengaged," indicating they are unhappy and unproductive at work and liable to spread negativity to co-workers. In rough numbers, this translates into 900 million not engaged and 340 million actively disengaged workers around the globe.

We seem to have a crisis of well-being in the workplace, where so few people get so little meaning out of their work.

What could be done to improve the conditions of well-being in the workplace and raise the statistic on the percentage of workers who experience meaning and joy from their work? Could workplace well-being be as important as profit maximization for business owners, CEOs and boards of directors?

Yes! By placing well-being at the heart of the role of doing business. This would require establishing corporate legal documents that express the "best interests" of the corporation in terms of well-being impacts on employees, the community and the environment.

From the happiness research, we know that meaningful work is one of the most important contributors to a happy life. Therefore, such low levels of engagement among global workers is clearly hindering economic productivity and life quality throughout much of the world.

Businesses that Operate on Well-Being Principles

Businesses can operate on a well-being framework. The very legal document—the corporate charter—that gives life to the corporation could be modified by inserting goals related to well-being impacts in section 3 of the corporate document, called Best Interests. The fact that most lawyers will leave this important section of the corporation's legal document blank, without any mention of responsibility for impacts, means there is an opportunity to express unequivocally the best interest of the firm or enterprise is to contribute to the well-being of employees, shareholders, the community and the environment.

This could represent a tectonic shift in the corporate law and the nature of business.

The emergence of the new B (Benefit) Corp. is a welcome sign that a new generation of business leaders are emerging that see their role in society as a force for good. B Corps are for-profit companies certified by the nonprofit B-Lab and registered in the State of Delaware. To certify, a B-Corp must meet rigorous standards of social and environmental performance, accountability, and transparency. Today, there are more than 1,600 Certified B Corps from 42 countries and over 120 industries working together toward the unifying goal of redefining success in business.

The Well-Being Corporation

I envision yet another progression beyond the B-Corp, that is, the well-being corporation. The well-being corporation would be governed by a set of asset management and accounting protocols require the enterprise to demonstrate net positive well-being impacts on society from its business operations. The board of directors would be responsible for assessing whether net positive negative or neutral impacts on well-being have been achieved on a regular reporting basis. A new generation of auditors will emerge to assess the well-being impacts of the enterprise on a broader suite of characteristics. A revised set of Generally Accepted Well-Being Accounting Principles (GAWAP) would be required, based however on a broader definition of both tangible and intangible assets, as defined in the five-asset model.

Doing Well By Doing Good: The Flourishing Well-Being Enterprise

The *Flourishing Enterprise* (2014)[2] presents a compelling new vision of the future enterprise based on the notion of flourishing and thriving. The authors suggest that flourishing—the aspiration that humans and life in general will thrive on the planet forever—should be a key goal for every business today. This is a bold concept. Just as sustainability has become part of the business lexicon, the principle of flourishing may become the newest aspiration for businesses.

Their hypothesis is that the quality of connectedness (increased consciousness) to the self, to others and to nature is essential for business to thrive. They argue that spirituality is at play in producing individual flourishing and is directly linked to value creation, which is also connected to stewardship. These authors point to a growing spiritual consciousness amongst corporate leaders such as John Mackay, co-founder of Whole Foods and author of *Conscious Capitalism*, who believes business leaders need to possess higher emotional and spiritual intelligence, help their employees feel self-actualization (Maslow's highest need in his hierarchy) and effectively help everyone win.

Their premise is that business could be oriented not simply to making money and maximizing profits for shareholders but to contribute the pursuit of well-being. Whether the pursuit of self-actualization and spiritual well-being can ever become the primary credo of business is for most a dubious aspiration and impossible dream. Yet some in the business world are trying to make happiness their highest goal for both their employees and customers.

One of the first companies to adopt happiness as its credo was Tony Hshieh's Zappos (one of the largest online shoe stores, acquired by Amazon in 2009). Tony believes that corporations can do well for their employees, customers and shareholders by following a higher purpose that transcends profits. He believes in creating a workplace where individuals and teams are allowed to figure out their "higher calling" and "higher purpose." For Zappos, the pursuit of a shared higher purpose led to success of the enterprise.

The late Ray Anderson of Interface Inc., the world's largest manufacturer of modular carpet, was a pioneer of the well-being enterprise, adopting a new corporate mantra: "Doing well by doing good." Anderson questioned the fundamental premise that profit maximization was the primary goal of a corporation. He experienced his own corporate epiphany when realized that the production of interior carpets by his company resulted in unaccounted future negative well-being impacts on people and the environment. Compelled by a sense of moral conviction, he led his company to create carpets that mimicked natural ecosystems (internalizing externalities of waste and pollution) and changing the nature of carpet as a product for purchase to something that provides service and whose utility would be leased from his company.

Ray mapped out the complex interrelationships of inputs and outputs, of resources, employees, suppliers, local communities, and pollutant releases to the environment. His full lifecycle analytic map was used to identify those relationships Interface had with all its stakeholders to ensure they no longer resulted in negative well-being impacts. Anderson was not motivated by money but from a sense of moral and social responsibility.

If Ray Anderson were alive today, he would surely be a champion of the flourishing enterprise or well-being corporation I am proposing. I have redrawn Anderson's original Interface model for the new 21st-century enterprise (Figure 33), incorporating the integrated-five capital asset model and Indigenous medicine wheel into the model. The result is a model of an enterprise that is conscious of the impacts of maintaining healthy and flourishing relationships amongst a multitude of stakeholders, with a view of past, present and future generational equity and relationships.

The model shows that each relationship can be represented by a line between two nodes or two entities or between each of the five capital assets of the enterprise. The integrity (wholeness) of these interrelationships can be measured in quantitative and qualitative terms. The most important of the qualitative metrics of integrity would be trust. The more trust between two people or two entities, the greater the transactional efficiency and effectiveness and the lower the cost of doing business. Imagine the length and thickness of the relational-trust line representing the flourishing nature of this relationship; the shorter and thicker that line between two entities, e.g., between corporate management and employees, the higher the degree of employee trust of senior management, which translates into lower turnover rates, fewer sick days and higher productivity

These relational integrity qualities can be measured, inventoried and accounted for within conventional accounting standards using similar accounting protocols used by financial accountants. An inventory or assessment of the integrity of relationships and thus well-being can be measured through objective quantitative measures as well as using subjective indicators such as surveys of employee well-being and customer relationships. Both objective and subjective indicators of relationships within

33 The Sustainable Enterprise Model: Interface Inc.

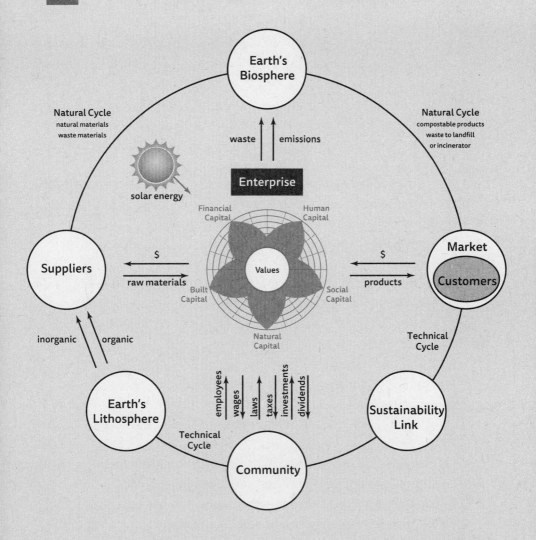

SOURCE: Based on the Interface model developed by Ray C. Anderson in *Mid-Course Correction: Toward Sustainable Enterprise* 1998. Chelsea Green Publishing.

this integral asset accounting and reporting system can be accounted for and summarized into an enterprise well-being index that would serve as a complement to conventional financial performance measures such as IRR, ROI, ROA, debt-asset ratio, and risk analysis.

Well-Being: The Best Interest of Business

Making well-being the ultimate bottom line of success for any business or any organization is to me the ultimate mountain peak of business success. Common sense would suggest that it should be given the importance of relationships and trust to the resilience and long-term financial success of any business enterprise. Measuring these relationships and the level of trust between the business enterprise and its customers, workers and the environment is the highest order of responsibility.

Embedding well-being into the aspirations and corporate legal charter (namely, the best interests of the enterprise) is perhaps the ultimate goal of 21st-century business culture.

Imagine if Section 3 of a corporation's legal charter read as follows:

+ *The Corporation* exists to provide well-being benefits to its partners, employees, clients, the communities in which it operates and the natural environment or ecosystem in which it operates.
+ *The Corporation* shall have the right to name specific public benefits, namely returns to well-being.
+ The creation of well-being and happiness, as a form of public benefit, is in the best interests of *The Corporation*.

These best interests would guide decision-making by the corporation's board of directors and senior management. The corporation's auditor would examine the financial statements and annual well-being impact report, expressing their opinion (the auditor's statement)[3] about a simple unequivocal question:

Do we believe the Corporation contributed to a net positive, neutral or negative well-being impact on the employees, shareholders, suppliers, the broader community and the natural environment in this fiscal operating period?'

We can envision a future where a new set of Generally Accepted *Well-Being* Accounting Principles would guide a new era of auditors. These auditors would express opinion on the long-term resilience and sustainability of the enterprise in terms of the five capital assets of the firm, not simply financial and other tangible assets.

Consider that corporations who produce an annual sustainability report often retain an accounting firm to express an opinion on the validity of their sustainability reporting, in the absence of a GAAP-like handbook for consistent accounting and reporting. The objective of the sustainability report auditor is to form a reasonable basis for his or her conclusion that the sustainability report provides a reliable and adequate presentation of the reporting organization's policy for sustainable development, as well as the activities, events and performance of the organization relating to sustainable development in a reporting period. These same standards could be applied to future well-being annual reporting.

I believe that companies that aspire to and embed well-being impacts into their corporate governance and human resources policies will be the most successful in the business world. These companies known that relationships are the key to a flourishing and vibrant enterprise and, ultimately, to long-term financial sustainability.

I envision companies with balance sheets that include an account of relational capital measured in terms of client satisfaction and trust, employee trust and employee engagement in the workplace. In addition, I envision companies reporting annually, or even quarterly, on their ecological or environment footprint in terms of how much land, resources, carbon and water they consume in the production of goods and services. This will include an accounting of the environmental impacts of their production, including water footprint analysis and land and carbon impact accounting. Mature companies will ultimately include such impact metrics in their product labeling and in their product and service pricing. These flourishing enterprises will take responsibility, as Ray Anderson did at Interface, for all of the relationships of business has with the multitude of stakeholders including the environment.

Boards of directors and investors would also become more conscious by expanding the current belief in the primacy of shareholder value and profit maximization to include the higher calling of care-holder[4] well-being. Board governance would adjust to consider the well-being impacts on current and future generations of all impacted by the activities of the enterprise, whether publicly traded or privately owned. Thus a culture of the primacy of care-holder well-being would become the operating norm.

These new corporations would thus become conscious (aware) of their well-being impacts both internally and externally. They would aspire to consider "doing well by doing good" and would contribute, in a measurable fashion, to the net positive well-being impact on society and the communities in which they operate. The result would be the emergence of a business culture infused with the Hippocratic oath to "do no harm" and to improve the world's state of well-being.

A Corporate Culture of Well-Being

The word *value* comes from the Latin word *valorum*, which means "to be worthy" or "to be strong." To adopt the culture of well-being suggested that we understand that genuine value and genuine strength in a culture will be one in which well-being is a central organizing principle and ultimate aspiration or mission of any organization.

A culture of well-being would put well-being at the center of all operating principles for the organization. What would these well-being principles be?

Father William Byron, a Jesuit priest who teaches business ethics and business in society at Saint Joseph's University in Philadelphia, suggests businesses adopt the following 14 principles for good corporate ethics in his book *The Power of Principles: Ethics for the New Corporate Culture* (2006, Orbis Books):

1. **Integrity:** Wholeness, solidity of character, honesty, trustworthiness, and responsibility.
2. **Veracity:** Telling the truth in all circumstances; accountability and transparency.

3. **Fairness:** Treating equals equally, giving to everyone his or her due.

4. **Human Dignity:** Acknowledging each person's inherent worth; respectful recognition of another's value simply for being human.

5. **Commitment:** Dependability, reliability, fidelity, loyalty and consistency.

6. **Reciprocity:** Uninhibited sharing of ideas with another member/partner without expecting anything in return.

7. **Financial compensation based on work effort:** Financial compensation may be in the form of either income or dividends depending on the desired form of financial compensation of each director

8. **Wage solidarity and maximum equity** (e.g., limit to ratio of top-bottom billable rates).

9. **Equitable distribution of financial residual** (surplus) in proportion to trade.

10. **Subsidiarity:** No decision should be taken at a higher level that can be made as effectively and efficiently at a lower level in the organization, with respect for proper autonomy.

11. **Cooperative One-Share-One-Vote:** Each director of the corporation has one share with one vote on all decisions: democratic control (one person/partner, one vote) and governance based on cooperation, shared responsibility, and using a circle, consensus-based decision-making process.

12. **Social Responsibility:** An obligation to look to the interest of the broader community and to treat the community as a stakeholder in what the enterprise does.

13. **Common Good:** Alignment of one's personal interests with the community's well-being: shared sense of purpose and responsibility for the common-wealth (well-being) of each other, the community and the environment. Contracts are with society for the purpose of improving well-being conditions.

14. **Love:** An internalized conviction that prompts a willingness to sacrifice one's time, convenience and a share of one's ideas and material goods for the good of others.

These principles could easily be adopted in all levels of governance and decision-making. To do so would help ensure that the orientation of the enterprise would be toward the higher aspiration of well-being. This would mean a corporate culture where the examination of conscience (self-reflective) in alignment with well-being operating principles would become normalized from the board of directors down to front-line workers. The aspiration of a flourishing, resilient and happier world of commerce would be possible.

Well-Being By Design

An intriguing aspect of the well-being economy would be application to architecture, design and building. What if buildings, schools, neighborhoods and entire cities were designed and built with well-being impact in mind? I've tested this concept with some friends who are architects, designers and in the construction industry. As some note, attributing well-being impacts to design may be difficult, given too many confounding variables.

London-based architect and designer Ilse Crawford seems to feel that well-being can be the basis of good design and construction. Ilse is the founder of the Man and Well-Being department at Design Academy Eindhoven in the Netherlands. She is also the author of the book *Sensual Home*, which was recently featured in the Netflix Series *Abstract*. In the series, Crawford talks about designing a building that is explicitly oriented to orchestrating feelings of well-being of the occupants. She believes that well-being is now beginning to permeate design schools that are realizing that the importance of people and their aspirations for quality of life and happiness comes first.

Crawford is keenly attuned to how design quality affects life and well-being on an everyday basis.[5] Crawford believes in making the ordinary extraordinary. She states, "I really do want well-being, the sense of physical and emotional health, to affect as many people as possible" and hopes this becomes "contagious."[6]

I believe Crawford's attempt to link design and well-being is of great importance to the world of architecture and design. Many of us can remember walking into a home or building or neighbor-hood and experiencing feelings of ease, comfort and even joy. What is it about the design of a space that elicits these feelings of well-being? Can buildings be intentionally designed to optimize experiences of well-being by their occupants? Will the current new sustainable building standards, including LEED certifica-tion,[7] IPD (integrated project delivery) and Lean manufacturing,[8] take the next step forward to well being by design?

Design based on well-being impacts will require new tools, measurable tools, including a well-being tape measure, to provide the objective skills to design with well-being impacts in mind. New standards for building design with well-being impacts in mind could emerge, similar to LEED (Leadership in Energy and Environmental Design) green building, homes and neighborhood design, construction and operations standards. For example, Isle Crawford has worked for IKEA looking at design attributes to make things and life better for families; helping IKEA design products that are both sustainable and something people love.

Crawford strives to infuse design—in both the visible and physical sense—with what she calls emotional values. She's more focused on life than on style. She says: "When I look at making spaces, I don't just look at the visual. I'm much more interested in the sensory thing, in thinking about it from the human context, the primal perspective, the thing that touches you." Whether the building is a new school, a hospital, a seniors' home or a family home, well-being attributes can be incorporated into the design features. An audit of the well-being impacts of design can be con-ducted on those who then work in or occupy the future space by asking simple questions about what they experience or feel about their work space, the building and other features of the workplace interior that they would attribute to their feelings of workplace well-being. I believe that paying attention to well-being attributes of interior spaces has a direct positive impact on the mental, physical, emotional and spiritual well-being of the space's users or occupants. These impacts can be measured in subjective terms by inquiring into the lived experience of the occupants. Design features that contribute to subjective well-being can then become considerations for architects, designers and builders.

These are ideas championed in the 1970s by architect Christopher Alexander in his seminal work *A Pattern Language* (1977). Alexander examined over 253 patterns in design and saw that when taken together they formed a language. Alexander viewed these patterns as a problem that could be solved, giving ordinary people a way to work with their neighbors to improve a town or neighborhood, design a house for themselves or work with colleagues to design an office, workshop or public building such as a school. At the core of Alexander's proposal was the idea that people should design their own houses, streets and communities. This idea comes from the observation that most of the wonderful places of the world were not made by architects but by the people.[9]

In Edmonton, Tom Redl, CEO of Chandos Construction, has been pioneering a new corporate culture based on a cooperative employee ownership model with shared responsibility, risk and financial benefits. The result has been steady growth in construction projects, highly functional teams, happy employees and high client satisfaction.

Chandos' mission is bold:

> To be the most innovative and progressive contractor in Canada. Our team aspires to identify and deliver value better than all others. We quite simply believe that we build better together. While the other guys worry about their piece of the pie, we work on making the pie bigger so that everyone can have a piece.[10]

Tom has championed the adoption of the IPD (integrated project delivery) model for Chandos and challenges his construction industry peers in Alberta to do the same. IPD brings more order, lower project costs and on-time-on-budget benefits to the construction industry. IPD is unique as it brings together all of the key players in a project from the architect, client, designers, building engineers, subcontractor and trades. IPD is a collaborative alliance of people, systems, business structures and practices in a process that harnesses the talents and insights of all participants to optimize project results, increase value to the owner, reduce waste and maximize efficiency through all phases of design, fabrication and construction. IPD is based on the Toyota production system (which also pioneered the Lean manufacturing system) and computer technology advances, with the integrated project delivery method focused on the final value created for the owner, the finished building.

Tom and I have discussed whether their new projects might incorporate well-being attributes and impacts into future Chandos projects. I suggested to Tom that well-being impacts on students and teachers might be incorporated into a new school Chandos was building in Red Deer, Alberta. This would include consideration of the choice of building materials, windows, doors and other attributes of the new school that would facilitate a positive sense of well-being and learning experience for students and teachers.

Notes

1. Ray Anderson was the champion of sustainability at Interface Ltd—the world's largest interior carpet manufacturer in Atlanta, Georgia.
2. Co-authored by Chris Laszlo and Judy Brown, with contributions from John R. Ehrenfeld, Mary Gotham, Ilma Barrow-Rose, Linda Robson, Roger Sallant, Dave Sherman and Paul Weader, and the foreword by Peter Senge.
3. In a typical audit, the accountant's letter usually expresses a "clean" opinion, which means the accountant or accounting firm believes the financial statements are accurate and that they fairly present the company's financial condition. A "qualified" opinion indicates deficiencies in the company's procedures or presentation (meaning the financial statements may not be accurate or may not conform to GAAP). An "adverse" opinion, which indicates that a company's financials are misrepresented, is yet another possibility. The most well-known opinion is the "going concern," which means that the accounting firm has doubts about the company's financial health and its ability to remain in business. Source: Investopedia.
4. The term "care-holder" was originally expressed to me by Rick Kohn, the former CFO of Mountain Equipment Co-op in Vancouver in 1999, in discussion about an integrated asset accounting model for companies. Rick was making a clear distinction between the traditional term

shareholder, referring to those individuals who own shares in a company, and all those impacted by an enterprise and its actions.

5. Christine Muhlke. "Profile in Style: Ilse Crawford". *The New York Times*. ISSN 0362-4331. September 25, 2008. Accessed June 26, 2016.

6. *Abstract. The Art of Design* on Netflix. 2017. itsnicethat.com/news /abstract-art-of-deign-netflix-series-190117. Accessed 2017.

7. LEED stands for Leadership in Energy and Environmental Design. LEED is a popular green building certification programs used worldwide, developed by the nonprofit US Green Building Council (USGBC). LEED includes a set of rating systems for the design, construction, operation and maintenance of green buildings, homes and neighborhoods that aims to help building owners and operators be environmentally responsible and use resources efficiently.

8. Lean manufacturing, or lean production, often simply "lean," is a systematic method for waste minimization within a manufacturing system without sacrificing productivity. Lean principles were derived from the Japanese manufacturing industry and pioneered by Toyota in the 1990s. Lean manufacturing reveals what adds value, by reducing everything else that does not add value.

9. Christopher Alexander, Sara Ishikawa, Murray Silverstein. *A Pattern Language*. Oxford University Press. 1977.

10. chandos.com/capabilities.php.

CHAPTER 7

Accounting for
Enterprise Well-Being

IF ECONOMISTS SHAPE the theology (beliefs and theories) of market capitalism, accountants determine what gets measured, reported and discussed amongst corporate executives and in board rooms.

Accounting standards define the manner in which all entities report on their financial performance and increasingly on their sustainability performance. Financial statements, including a balance sheet and income statement, are prepared annually to determine whether an enterprise generated a net profit or loss. These annual financial statements are key to determine payment of taxes to governments and dividends to shareholders. Yet not everything that matters gets counted, and not everything that gets counted matters particularly to well-being.

Could accountants begin to account for well-being performance and impact of an enterprise? Would accounting for well-being impacts ever become a normal state of practice for management, tax and audit accountants? I would suggest that is a possible future; indeed, I believe accounting for well-being impacts will change the world of accountancy that has used the same standards for more than five hundred years. In my previous book, I traced the history of accounting back to 15th-century Venice, when Franciscan mathematician Fra Luca Bartolomeo de Pacioli (c. 1447–1517) and his student of mathematics Leonardo da Vinci (c. 1452–1519) developed the double-entry accounting system still used today by professional accountants.

If Pacioli's notion of debits=credits and the balance sheet was inspired by nature's design (the golden mean and the Fibonacci sequence of numerical progression), then why can't we conceive of an accounting system that measures a broader suite of assets? The fact that Pacioli never defined the word *profit* in a formal bookkeeping sense suggests that alternative bottom-line measures of success may one day include measures of well-being impacts and a well-being return on assets and investments.

Ronnie Lessem, a new colleague and a former articling chartered accountant who is South African, wrote a seminal paper in 1973 titled "Accounting for an Enterprise's Wellbeing."[1] In reading Lessem's brilliant article I realized that the notion of the well-being enterprise and accounting had already been identified more than 44 years earlier. Lessem has moved on from accounting and has spent his prolific scholarly life on an "integral model" for economies and finance. His integral view of the world is nearly identical to the Indigenous model of the medicine wheel and four directions, and complementary to my five-capital-asset model. Lessem's vision is to integrate the best of economic thought and models from the four worlds: north, south, east and west. His thesis is that the world has been dominated by the economics of northern cultures while Indigenous cultures, particular those from Africa and North America, have had virtually no traction in the modern world of economics, accounting and finance. Ronnie and I, along with Robert Dellner, an investment banker based in London, are now in regular discussions about how to advance the ideas and principles of well-being economics and finance using the integral approach.

In Lessem's early work, he attempted to "extend fundamental accounting principles, which have traditionally embraced only monetary stocks and flows, towards physical, social and psychological exchanges." His paper puts forward the notion of quality-of-life accounting, based, in part on Abram Maslow's hierarchy of needs combined with conventional accounting rules. He provides a foundation for the development of a new generation of accountants/auditors beyond their traditional role of audit and tax accounting to a new era of management accounting in an era of growing interest in social and environmental responsibility and impact investment. Lessem's accounting system "does not attempt to develop thoroughgoing quantitative measures to the same degree of specificity as conventional financial accounts; rather it aims to develop a novel framework, to which both management practitioners and theorists may apply their own specific refinements."

This important work provides the intellectual foundations for a new generation of accountants who would specialize in enterprise-well-being accounting in both the private and public sector accounting worlds.

The Origins of Auditing

As Lessem notes, auditing is a practice within the accounting discipline that has its origins in the 19th century, at the time of the Industrial Revolution with an emphasis on the economic wealth of nations. This was a time when the control of vast sums of money necessitated internal controls, or accounting standards. The balance sheet was useful for providing the true and fair value of the state of affairs of a business and where bookkeeping became the systematic recording of transactions or exchange of value, either in the form of money or of goods and services measured in terms of money.

Could accounting standards of valuation, inventory, balance sheets and income statements extend beyond simple money measures of value to attributes of assets that constitute impacts on individual, household, community and environmental well-being?

Toward Quality-of-Life Auditing and Accounting

Dr. R. E. Walton, director of research at Harvard Business School in 1972, envisioned a day when there would be a reordering of values away from productivity, technology and growth toward equalization of wealth and opportunity, self-expression and human contact, and an appreciation of the earth's natural endowments.[2]

Walton might agree that such a reordering would necessitate a new accounting approach to support the modern business corporation with a well-being mandate and ethic.

As early as the 1950s, Rensis Likert, director of the Social Research Institute at the University of Michigan, had pioneered a move toward "human asset accounting."[3,4] Likert's basic proposition was that human resources within organizations should be considered as assets and accounted for accordingly. Eric Flamholtz would go on to develop a precise methodology to value an individual according to his productivity and transferability alongside his potential earnings stream.[5]

Lessem goes a step further, suggesting a system of quality-of-life audit and accounting protocols that integrates physical, economic, social and psychological factors, many of which cannot be represented in financial or money terms.

Lessem draws on Abram Maslow's hierarchy of needs model for his quality-of-life accounting system combined with the accounting principles of double entry. Double entry recognizes that with any interrelationship or transaction there is a two-fold aspect, namely, the receipt of something of monetary value (or non-monetary) by one person and the parting with it by another. This is the notion of a debit balancing a credit. As Lessem notes, a double-entry relationship is at play in all aspects of life:

> In a marital relationship affection may be exchanged between husband and wife whereby the medium of exchange is love and both giver and receiver are affected; in our ecological system, a bee interacts with a flower whereby the medium of exchange is pollen and again both giver and receiver are affected. In this instance the plant is "debited" and the insect "credited" for the receipt incurred.

My challenge to Lessem is whether double-entry relationship accounting can work without cash accounting or monetizing each debt-credit relationship. If so, this would open up a new chapter in asset and transactional accounting where each debt and credit relationship would be defined in terms of a net positive impact to the well-being of an interrelationship.

Well-Being Inventory

Every audit process begins with a physical inventory of the various assets of the business enterprise. In the case of well-being-asset inventory this would involve a listing of events or transactions which characterize the relationships between the corporation and the community and natural environment. The inventory would entail defining the contributions or impacts (positive, neutral or negative) the corporation has on the environment (e.g., pollution, carbon footprint, water footprint) employees, customers and the general community.

The well-being model uses a physical and qualitative inventory of the enterprise's five assets using the proposed suite of well-being indicators as proxies of the overall integrity and state of resilience of each of the five capital assets and their interrelationship. The inventory reveals both the strengths (integrity) and weaknesses (risks or liabilities) of each asset class. Measures of integrity can be developed using a numeric scoring system verified by expert opinion.

The relationship between the enterprise and the various stakeholders impact can be mapped in a relational-life-cycle model of Ray Anderson's Interface that accounts for the interrelationship and relative impact of an enterprise on employees, the community and the natural environment. The interrelationship between the enterprise and other stakeholders can be measured in units of trust or integrity using survey tools and other proxies of trust. The units of measurement to assess the complex interrelationships and flows will require a number of measurement units, including physical (material), energy, socio-psychological (e.g., trust), financial and consciousness (e.g., perceptions). Many of these non-monetary units of measure will require continuous testing, verification and benchmarking.

Five Assets of Enterprise Well-Being

Lessem points out that an asset is usually defined, in strict accounting terms, as "some form of property which the business possesses." The more general definition of the term comes from

from the Latin *ad satis*, meaning "to sufficiency" or having sufficient potential to discharge, pay or compensate for some burden, debt or liability.

The term *liability*, in conventional accounting terms, is defined as "a debt owing by the business," from the original Latin *liabilis*, meaning "that can be bound." A liability is therefore referring to being bound to someone or owing something.

An asset is therefore something that could yield future satisfaction or utility to the owner, while a liability is something that could result in disutility. For example, a piece of equipment purchased by a manufacturer can provide the basis of the production of a commodity and its sale to provide sufficient money flows or cash returns. Another example is a tree or an acre of farm land; these are forms of natural capital assets that could yield future satisfaction to the owner in the form of timber from the tree's harvest or food produced from the land. There are other forms of assets that extend into non-monetary intangibles such as relationships, trust, and goodwill.

Lessem notes

> the whole concept of the balance sheet applies more to potential rather than actual performance. In the process of analyzing a company's particular gearing or liquidity ratio one is essentially passing judgment on its capacity to perform in the future. Moreover, the store of utility or disutility inherent in the assets and liabilities of an enterprise are only potentially convertible into streams of income and expenditure, profit and loss.

Lessem proposed in 1973 a quality-of-life accounting system based on Maslow's hierarchy of needs. Using Maslow's model suggests there may be pre-conditions for physiological survival that will include ecological integrity (e.g., water and air quality).

Lessem's quality-of-life accounting model is based on the:

> underlying accounting principles related to an organization's membership which may be linked to the various

quality of life categories (Maslow) so as to facilitate an integrated auditing procedure that gives a true and fair view of the physical, economic and socio-psychological state of the affairs of the business.[6]

My proposed integrated five-asset model adopts standard accounting conventions (inventory, asset and liability accounting, and the balance sheet), however, through a lens of well-being performance and impacts of the enterprise in relationship with the community and the natural world. The complex interrelationships among numerous assets of the enterprise are mapped, inventoried and assessed in terms of a new bottom line of well-being outcomes, sufficiency and impacts. At the same time liabilities or risks to future well-being are accounted for and managed accordingly. Therefore, utility or well-being impact of an asset becomes the central focus of accounting and thus auditing.

I propose at least five asset classes for the well-being enterprise or organization, applied to either private, public or nonprofit sectors. The five asset accounts would include a robust set of well-being asset sub-accounts or criteria as per Figure 34. The individual indicators of enterprise well-being are proposed as proxies of well-being conditions of each of the five capital assets of an enterprise or business. Many of these indicators are consistent with the Global Reporting Initiative (GRI) sustainability accounting and reporting guidelines used by many companies to produce sustainability reports.

The five capital asset accounts for an enterprise can be described as follows, with more detailed attributes or sub-asset accounts:

Human capital asset accounts include people's health, happiness, skills, education, knowledge and the amount of time they have available to contribute to societal well-being. This class also includes intellectual capital, including ideas and innovation. Human capital also involves the balanced use of time to fulfill basic human needs such as fulfilling employment, spirituality, understanding, skills development, creativity and freedom. The

34 | Enterprise Well-Being Assets

Financial Capital

Financial Assets
- Current financial assets
  - Cash
  - Accounts receivable
  - Inventories
- Capital assets

Financial Liabilities
- Debt (short- and long-term borrowings)
- Accounts payable

Shareholders' Equity
- Preferred securities
- Share capital
- Retained earnings

Built Capital

- Infrastructure
  - Roads
  - Pipelines
  - Transmission lines
  - Other structures
- Buildings
- Machinery and equipment
- Technology
- Patents
- Brands
- Intellectual property (ideas, innovations)
- Management processes
- Production processes
- Databases

Natural Capital

- Environmental goods and services
- Natural resources (stocks and flows)
  - Land
  - Minerals
  - Oil, gas, coal
  - Forests (trees)
  - Fish and wildlife
  - Water
  - Air
  - Carbon sinks
- Ecosystem integrity
- Energy (by type, source, and end-use)

Human Capital

- People (employees, contractors, suppliers)
- Intellectual capital
  - Educational attainment
  - Knowledge
  - Skills
- Employment rate
- Labor participation rates
- Full-time, permanent job rate
- Benefits including workplace interventions
- Creativity and entrepreneurship
- Capabilities
- Motivation
- Productivity
- Happiness (self-rated)
- Time use balance (work, family, leisure, comunity)
- Health (diesease, diet, overall health)
- Physical well-being (fitness)
- Mental well-being
- Spiritual well-being
- Addictions (drugs, alcohol, gambling)
- Workplace safety
- Training and professional development
- Personal self-development

Social Capital

- Customer relationships (value, loyalty and commitment by customers)
- Supplier relationships (value and commitment by suppliers
- Reputation
- Workplace relational capital
  - Employee interrelationships
  - Workplace climate (e.g., stress, excitement, joy)
  - Social cohesion (teams and team spirit)
- Equity (incomes, age-sex distribution, women in management)
- Employee family quality of life
- Networks
- Friendships amongst workplace colleagues
- Membership in professional associations, clubs
- Social events with colleagues
- Family outings with workplace colleagues
- Financial investment, giving and donations

SOURCE: Anielski Management Inc. 2017.

important assets in this capital class are intangible; they include the many forms of knowledge assets and important relationship-based assets such as employee and customer equity.

+ People (employees, contractors, suppliers)
+ Educational attainment, knowledge and skills
+ Percentage of workers earning a living wage
+ Perceived fair pay index
+ Full-time and part-time employees
+ Employees with full benefits
+ Employees with pension plans
+ Meaningful work index (employee self-rated)
+ Life satisfaction index
+ Health (physical, mental, spiritual) index
+ Work-life balance index
+ Workplace well-being index
+ Workplace relationships index
+ Workplace trust index (employer, colleagues, management)
+ Belonging index
+ Satisfaction with personal and professional development
+ Workplace safety index

Social and cultural capital includes the strength of relationships, associations, networks and levels of trust people have for each other particularly in the workplace, with work-related customers and with members of the community. Social capital includes the web of interpersonal connections, social networks, cultural heritage, traditional knowledge and the institutional arrangements, rules, norms and values that facilitate human interactions and cooperation between people. These contribute to social cohesion; strong, vibrant, and secure communities; and good governance and help fulfill basic human needs such as participation, affection and a sense of belonging. The social capital class asset include:

+ Customer relationship value: Life-time customer value (LCV)
+ Trust index: employee-management and stakeholder (customers, suppliers)
+ Customer lists

+ Supply chain relationships: supplier value, supply agreements
+ Workplace well-being index
+ Fair and equitable distribution of income, age-sex distribution, women in management.
+ Employee family quality of life
+ Networks
+ Friendships amongst workplace colleagues
+ Family outings with workplace colleagues
+ Membership in professional associations, clubs or other organizations
+ Social events with colleagues
+ Financial investment/giving/donations to the community
+ Social license to operate

I would argue that trust is the most important of all social assets. Stephen M. Covey notes in his book *The Speed of Trust* that to be trusted is the most profound feature of human motivations. Yet you won't find trust on the balance sheet of an enterprise or organization, other than a proxy called goodwill, which is an inadequate monetary estimate of relational capital value.

Measuring trust is possible with customer value audits. Using survey tools and an interview process, the level of trust, integrity and quality of the interrelationship between the business and clients can be measured.

Natural capital includes the land, water and ecological goods and services that nature provides free of charge for human well-being and that are used or damaged in the process of business activities. The natural environment is the source capital for all other forms of wealth. Its biodiversity and ecosystems are the goods and services by which humanity survives and thrives. These goods and services are essential to basic needs such as survival, climate regulation, habitat for other species, water supply, food, fiber, fuel, recreation, cultural amenities and the raw materials required for all economic production. The assets embedded within this capital class are both tangible and intangible. Oil and gas, grains, timber and other traditional resources have established asset parameters and capitalization schedules. Many other assets in this capital class deliver non-exchange well-being benefits. For example, clean air, and fresh water are vital to wellbeing; the well-being-accounting model treats them like the real assets they are, for the first time providing them visibility in terms of formal treatment.

+ Industrial footprint (area of land used)
+ Water footprint (water use per unit of production and sales)
+ Environmental footprint
+ Carbon footprint
+ Environmental goods and services
+ Energy use
+ Natural resource reserves (timber, agricultural soil, oil, gas, minerals)

Built capital includes anything that is manufactured, including tangible assets such as buildings, equipment and software as well as intangible assets such as patents, trademarks, models, ideas, knowledge and business processes created through the combination of human, social and natural capital assets. The intangible asset revolution of the 21st century is rapidly expanding the asset potential of knowledge, particularly in the realm of patentable inventions, copyrightable materials and network applications of various kinds—which now dominate advanced economies. Built capital assets include

+ Buildings, real estate
+ Plant & equipment
+ Land
+ Land improvements
+ Inventory
+ Supplies (less accumulated depreciation)
+ Intangible built assets
+ Patented innovations and business processes
+ Brands (including trade dress, mastheads, unique color, shape, package designs
+ Trademark

+ Trade secrets (formulas, processes, recipes)
+ Computer software
+ Non-patented technology
+ Databases
+ Intangible contract-based assets
+ License agreements
+ Royalty contracts
+ Franchise agreements
+ Development rights agreements (oil, water, timber)
+ Service contracts

Financial capital includes traditional financial assets as well as liabilities and shareholder/stakeholder equity that make up an entity community or municipality. These include
+ Cash
+ Investments
+ Accounts receivable
+ Prepaid insurance
+ Debt
+ Liabilities (conventional)
+ Liabilities (unfunded: social, environmental)
+ Equity (distribution of financial assets)

Measuring Workplace Well-Being

Valuing workplace well-being is beginning to emerge as well. According to a Gallup research paper by Tom Rath and Jim Harter (coauthors of *Wellbeing: The Five Essential Elements*),

> Whether you manage a few people, lead a large group, or run an entire organization, you are already in the business of managing employee wellbeing. The research on this topic is quite clear: Your workforce's wellbeing has a direct impact on your organization's bottom line. Even if you have never thought of your employees' wellbeing as "your business," each person's wellbeing is critical to achieving an organization's goals and fulfilling its mission.

Just as the most successful organizations have worked systemically to optimize their levels of employee engagement in recent decades, they are now turning their attention to employee well-being as the way to gain an emotional, financial, and competitive edge.

Rath and Harter have defined five essential elements of well-being in the workplace:

1. **Career Wellbeing:** how you occupy your time and liking what you do each day.
2. **Social Wellbeing:** having strong relationships and love in your life.
3. **Financial Wellbeing:** effectively managing your economic life to reduce stress and increase security.
4. **Physical Wellbeing:** having good health and enough energy to get things done on a daily basis.
5. **Community Wellbeing:** the sense of engagement and involvement you have with the area where you live.

Combining the strings of the Rath and Harter five well-being elements model, the 1989 Brundtland Commission's Sustainable Livelihoods Model and the Indigenous medicine wheel, I have devised a Well-Being Workplace measurement system (i.e., survey and reporting tools) that allows individuals, teams and the entire enterprise to self-assess the strengths of their five-personal assets.

Employee well-being and overall workplace well-being can be scored on a scale of 0–100 across several personal well-being domains. A 20-question Workplace Well-Being Survey tool is used, with individuals and teams self-assessing key questions about personal well-being and workplace well-being. The survey results are converted into scores that are then used to create an index (Figure 35) image that is a stylized well-being index in the shape of a spider graphic with a flower image as wallpaper. Individuals can choose any type of flower image or other image to color their personal well-being index.

35   The Employee Well-Being Index

SOURCE: Anielski Management Inc. 2017.

The individual employee and Workplace Well-Being Index provides a simple, visually striking well-being index in the shape of a flower, showing which aspects of an employee well-being are flourishing and which are not. Self-rated well-being is based on a numeric score of 1–100 for each well-being attribute, or flower pedal. The well-being flower clearly shows what areas (i.e., petals) of individual or workplace well-being are thriving and which ones need work. The example image shows a perfect state of flourishing well-being.

Each team or unit within an organization can be measured and profiled with a similar image and ultimately rolled up into a single Workplace Well-Being Index. The flower index is the ultimate image of resilience and flourishing of an organization. I envision well-being surveys and well-being indices becoming a common standard in the workplace in the assessing and reporting of conditions of workplace well-being.

Standardized self-rating of employee well-being can then be used to regularly calibrate workplace well-being by addressing both individual and team assets, competencies and areas for improvement. This will also help strengthen workplace consciousness or awareness within the organization of the conditions of well-being. This will help in team building as well as improving the relationships with customers and other stakeholders.

Enterprise Well-Being Index

Each of the five capital assets and their various attributes can be measured in quantitative and qualitative terms as well as monetary value terms. Each well-being indicator would be assigned a well-being score from 0 (zero integrity or poor well-being) to 100 (maximum well-being or flourishing integrity) that establishes a condition of each well-being measure (Figure 36). Qualitative scoring of assets is similar to how wines are rated in terms of quality using a scale of 0 to 100 to help consumers determine which wines to purchase.

In the well-being accounting model, relative well-being thresholds are established based on comparing or benchmarking performance across other firms, businesses or enterprises in similar

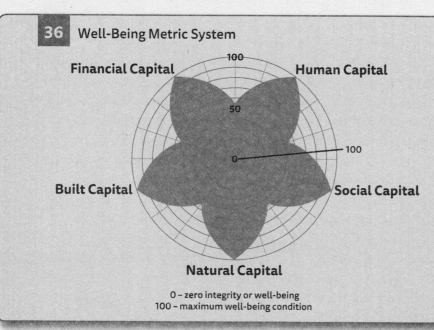

36 Well-Being Metric System

Financial Capital   100   Human Capital

50

0   100

Built Capital   Social Capital

Natural Capital

0 – zero integrity or well-being
100 – maximum well-being condition

SOURCE: Anielski Management Inc. 2017.

sectors, where data are publicly available and where comparison of performance results is possible. Comparative well-being performance data are drawn from sources such as Bloomberg, GRI reports, annual reports of firms (including sustainability reports) and other public sources.

Over time and with regular reporting and verification of this broader suite of assets, a common protocol for inventory and integrity measurement will emerge as such protocols have with 500 years of double-entry bookkeeping conventions

The composite enterprise well-being index would give management and decision-makers an overall well-being score that can be tracked over time. This will help to evaluate the current and long-term resiliency of the enterprise that is materially important to investors for making prudent investment decisions. Such protocols would be strengthening the capacity for a new generation of impact investors to assess investment opportunities and risk.

True Pricing: Full-Cost Accounting

One of the most important issues in business and economics is the determination of fair market value, or the true price of product or service.

Anthroposophist Rudolf Steiner developed the idea and core concept of a threefold social organism between 1917 and 1922. In it he recognized three domains of human social activity: economic, legal and cultural. Steiner maintained that the health of human society depended on an adult population that understood the characteristics of each domain and could thereby organize society so that each domain enjoyed independence and autonomy. In his economic lectures Steiner spoke about price setting by bringing together all stakeholders and parties involved. Steiner maintained that the entire economic life is encompassed by what he called the "Law of True Price." He formulated the law in these words: "A true price is forthcoming when a man receives, as counter-value for the product he has made, an amount sufficient to enable him to satisfy the whole of his needs, including of course the needs of his dependents, until he will again have completed a like product."[7]

The notion of sufficient compensation to enable the satisfaction of life's needs is similar to the notion of a living wage—a wage sufficient to satisfy one's needs for a good life. Calculating a true price for a product might be similar to the calculation of a living wage in any community.

Along the lines of Steiner's true price logic model, I employ full-cost accounting methods to determine the full suite of costs and benefits of an asset, program or service, with the view of calculating a well-being return on investment. This includes accounting for the value of intangible assets such as trust and relationships. Measuring the monetary costs and benefits associated with various assets deployed or impacted by an enterprise is similar to the Genuine Progress Indicator accounting model used to adjust national income accounts (i.e., GDP) for unaccounted benefits (e.g., unpaid work) and societal and environmental costs associated with economic output.

Making the Business Case of Well-Being

I have conducted several well-being impact and full-cost-benefit economic analysis studies for several clients over the past 15 years who have had an interest in making the business case for their programs. These include

* The Alberta Motor Association (similar to the CAA and AAA) in accounting for the well-being impacts of their traffic safety programs.
* Alberta Environment Ministry study of the societal well-being benefits of Alberta's recycling programs for bottles, tires, oil and electronics.
* A national socioeconomic analytic framework for assessing the well-being impacts of gambling in Canada, using a well-being impact analytic approach.[8]
* The well-being benefits and impacts of the B.C. Construction Association's program to provide skilled workers quicker access into B.C. construction trades and market.[9]
* Making a socio-ecological-economic business case for the conservation of wetlands by Ducks Unlimited Canada. The

study found that for every $1 invested in Ducks Unlimited
Canada conservation programs Canadians receive about $22
in well-being benefits, including 969 jobs, $59.6 million in
wages, $77.1 billion in GDP benefits, $208 million per year in
nature-related recreation benefits and $4.27 billion worth of
unpriced ecological services.[10]

+ A cost-benefit and well-being impact analysis of Alberta's
$1.2 billion affordable housing program measured in terms of
the subjective well-being impacts and economic cost-benefits
of the programs as experienced by beneficiaries.[11] The result
is the first study of its kind that produced a quantitative well-
being ROI that can be compared with conventional economic
(cost-benefit) and financial benefit measures.

The calculation of the value of wetland conservation and the treatment of wetlands as an asset for Ducks Unlimited Canada (DUC)
is instructive. DUC's financial statements contained an estimate
of the value of the 2.5 million acres of wetlands that this organization had conserved over its 75-year history. I informed the DUC
executive of the importance of accounting for wetlands as legitimate assets that belong on their balance sheet. In addition, they
had an opportunity to account for the societal well-being benefits
of wetlands to Canadians. I noted that Nature Conservancy Canada had begun to report the purchase value of its conservation
easement lands as assets on their balance sheet. While DUC's accountants had not previously prepared such a balance sheet, my
proposed accounting approach was supported by Joe Batty, a CA
and former CFO of NAIT (Northern Institute of Technology) in Edmonton. Joe noted that it was entirely within the scope of asset
accounting protocols and GAAP to evaluate the societal value of
a wetlands as a legitimate accounting practice to show their value
to donors and government funders. The result would be a significant increase in the overall assets (natural assets) on the balance
sheets of these conservation organizations.

A comprehensive calculation of the economic, employment
and ecological benefits (well-being ROI) of wetlands to the well-

being of Canadians was made. Wetlands, like most natural capital assets, are not counted on balance sheets of corporations or in public accounts of governments. Yet they provide critical non-monetized ecological services, including clean drinking water, flood mitigation and carbon bank accounts storing vast amounts of carbon in the atmosphere. Accounting for these values to society meant that DUC could now present revised financial statements to their donors, including governments, that showed the value of natural assets they conserved for the benefit of Canadians. I calculated that every $1 of government money invested in DUCs wetland conservation efforts had a seven-month return on investment in the form of tax revenues related to employment, business expenses and GST (goods and service taxes). The result was that DUC could now make the business case to all levels of governments and their donors that investing in wetland asset conservation delivered a net positive well-being ROI.

In a similar study, I was asked to calculate the societal value of the Alberta Motor Association's (AMA/CAA or AAA in the US) traffic safety programs. The analysis for the AMA involved the assessment of the true full cost of auto crashes in Alberta and the benefit of AMA's traffic safety programs and campaigns. I was able to calculate, through full-cost accounting methods, that each car crash-injury avoided would save society ten thousand dollars in related health care costs and other costs.

More recently I was part of a team of economic analysts that evaluated the cost-benefits and well-being impacts of Alberta's $1.2-billion affordable housing program (2008–12). The government of Alberta, prompted by a critique by the provincial auditor general, sought a conventional cost-benefit analysis of the affordable housing program. The auditor general was critical of the program for not being able to demonstrate its effectiveness. As economists, we are used to constructing cost-benefit ratios but have not been accustomed to assessing the effectiveness of programs. We proposed a well-being impact analytic tool to the government along with a conventional cost-benefit and capital efficiency analysis. The housing ministry liked our proposed analytic methods. The result was the ability of the government to demonstrate a positive well-being ROI of Alberta's affordable housing program, something that had never been done before.

Asset Valuation and Verification with Well-Being in Mind

Asset valuation and verification is the process of assessing the value of a company, real property or any other item of worth that produces cash flows. Asset valuation is commonly performed prior to the purchase or sale of an asset or prior to purchasing insurance for an asset. Asset valuation can be based on cash flows, comparable valuation metrics or transaction value.

I have found the concept of highest-and-best use valuations used in the real estate sector to be particularly compelling for application to the broader suite of asset valuation.

Normally, a real estate appraiser is acquainted with the Appraisal Institute definition of highest and best use. Under this definition, real estate is assessed based on the reasonably probable and legal use of vacant land or an improved property that is physically possible, reasonably permissible, appropriately supported, financially feasible and that results in the highest value. Highest and best use is determined based on the use of the asset by market participants, even if the intended use of the asset by the reporting entity is different—in broad terms, the use of an asset by market participants that would maximize the value of the asset or the group of assets within which the asset would be used.

I propose that similar highest and best use protocols be applied to human, social and cultural assets, as well as the full suite of built assets. Social assets such as trust would be evaluated using various methods to discern the strength of relationship (e.g., trust) amongst and between individuals and organizations in the community, between workers, and between a business and customers. Survey methods are used to determine levels of trust, sense of belonging and perceived levels of engagement in the workplace and the level of meaning derived from work. This would require defining how various assets deliver value for the

owners of assets and impacts stakeholders who receive the benefits of assets when utilized.

Asset valuation usually consists of both subjective and objective measurements, which is consistent with the well-being asset
accounting model used to measure the five assets of communities or organizations. For many intangible assets, such as a company's brand, customer value or employee engagement, there is
no financial number found on the financial statements that tells
investors how much these intangibles are worth. Nevertheless,
these assets can be evaluated from a subjective perspective using
alternative measures of integrity, trust and resilience, which become non-monetary proxies for the worth of these intangibles to
the long-term flourishing of the enterprise. I am also convinced
that with full-cost accounting efforts, intangibles such as employee engagement, customer value and trust can be linked to the
productivity of work teams, contracts and thus financial profit-
ability. There is a way of linking subjective measures of intangible
assets and objective measurement, namely income and expenses.
In this way these more complicated intangibles can be monetized,
with obvious caveats. That means that many of these once hidden
assets can and should be noted as valuable by management accountants inside companies, if not formally listed on the year-end
financial statements.

This would strengthen the capacity of analysts to expand the
assessment of the worth of a company beyond conventional market and replacement values of assets, with a deeper appreciation
of how natural, social and human capital assets contribute to the
long-term resilience and flourishing of the enterprise. I see this as
a new frontier in asset valuation and accounting that will provide
those early adopters of intangible asset accounting a competitive
advantage. A more comprehensive asset valuation should also
provide investment firms with an impact investment focus with
a comparative advantage over others as they can measure the
hidden and unaccounted treasures that lie hidden under conventional assets.

As with other disciplines in which assets and values or assessed, the well-being model requires verification by experts in their field to affirm the integrity and economic value of the various asset classes in the five-capital model.

Notes

1. Ronnie Lessen, "Accounting for an Enterprise's Wellbeing," *The Int. Jl of Mgmt Sci.*, Vol. 2, No. 1, 1974, The City University, London, England, 1973.
2. R. E. Walton, "Frontiers beckoning the organizational psychologist." *Journal of Applied Behavioral Science,* September 1972, 601–603.
3. R. Likert, *New Patterns of Management*. McGraw-Hill, New York, 1961.
4. R. Likert, *The Human Organization*. McGraw-Hill, New York, 1967.
5. E. Flamholtz, The Theory and Measurement of an Individual's Value. PhD Thesis, University of Michigan, 1969.
6. Ronnie Lessem, "Accounting for an Enterprise's Wellbeing," *The International Journal of Management Science*, Vol. 2, No. 1, 1974, The City University, London, England, 1969.
7. R. Steiner, *The Renewal of the Social Organism*, Anthroposophic Press, 1985.
8. Mark Anielski, *A Socio-Economic Impact of Gambling Framework*, Prepared for the Canadian Centre for Substance Abuse: 2008.
9. Anielski Management Inc. *A Well-Being Return on Investment Assessment of the BCCA Connector Models*. Report prepared for the BC Construction Association. September 2013.
10. Mark Anielski, John Thompson and Sara Wilson. *A Genuine Return on Investment: The Economic and Societal Well-Being Value of Land Conservation in Canada*. Prepared for Ducks Unlimited Canada. 2014.
11. This study was completed in 2016 for the Government of Alberta by SHS Consulting and our team of economists at Genuine Wealth Inc. The report has not yet been released publicly.

CHAPTER 8

Well-Being Impact Investing

*Man naturally desires, not only to be loved, but to be lovely; or
to be that thing which is the natural and proper object of love.
He naturally dreads, not only to be hated, but to be hateful; or to
be that thing which is the natural and proper object of hatred.*
—Adam Smith (*The Theory of Moral Sentiments*)

THE WORLD OF FINANCE, banking and investment would seemingly be the most challenging of all sectors to introduce a moral sentiment of well-being. Could the creation of money and the notion of wealth maximization be reoriented to the goal of improving well-being for the common good?

The financialization of the economy—an increase in the size and importance of a country's financial sector relative to its overall economy—has led to the commoditization and monetization of virtually all aspects of life, including the environment. This has led to a world of increasing individualism and materialism and a preoccupation with the self and a "what is good for me" attitude.

While Adam Smith's *The Wealth of Nations* provided the foundation stones of our modern economies and financial capitalism, his other work, *The Theory of Moral Sentiment*, gives us hope that human beings are predisposed to doing good for others. I believe business leaders are called to engage the contemporary financial world on the basis of the common good and an ethic of doing good for others. But how can this ethic of contributing to the well-being and good of the other be squared with the primacy of making money? How can the financial market economy mature into the well-being economy of shared assets with the goal of human flourishing?

What if business and financial activities are carried out justly and effectively, where customers receive goods and services at fair and true prices? What if employees felt valued and engaged in work that brought their lives meaning? What if employees felt a strong sense of belonging to their workplace and experienced a high-level of trust with clients? What if investors in the shares of corporations earned a reasonable return on their investment but also appreciated how their investments were contributing to the improved state of well-being of individuals, families, communities and the environment impacted by the corporations in which they invested? What if neighbors could help each other in their respective financial needs, sharing individual gifts and skills, and become each other's bankers, investing directly in the assets of our neighborhoods and communities?

Virtuous Financial Leadership

I see a new generation of business and financial leadership emerging who epitomizes a shift in the nature of banking and finance. Ken Costa is one of these champions, with over 40 years in the financial sector. He was born and raised in South Africa and studied philosophy and law in Johannesburg. Ken spent 30 years of his life as an investment-merchant banker in London, including serving as vice-chairman of UBS Investment Bank, a global financial institution, and as chairman of Lazard International, joining the bank in October 2007 and staying until 2011.

Ken is a champion of a new era of ethical finance and business. Ken's important book *God at Work*[1] provides a remarkable account of how his Christian faith has helped him to see the important opportunity for orienting the world of finance as a force for good. Ken understands that being a business leader and merchant banker is a unique and sometimes challenging vocation (calling) in which one must balance one's own ethics and morals with the primary onus of the financial industry for making money, sometimes at any cost. Ken is now a champion of a new generation of investment bankers who believe in the use the tools of finance for good.

Following a new ethic or moral sentiment toward well-being and the good of others in finance and banking is not without its challenges. Most would wonder if this is even possible without eventually selling your soul to the money power. Financial leaders like Ken Costa understand that it is important to remain part of the world and his learned world of investment banking to effect change within the system. As Ken notes, there came a moment in his life when he realized that his work station at the bank had become his worship station.

He realized that being an investment banker for good was as much as a calling as choosing to pursue a vocation as a priest or religious leader.

Investment for Good

Robert Dellner is a London-based investment banker who is pioneering a new generation of impact investment funds based on a philosophy that companies that strive to improve the lives of their employees, customers and society will ultimately outperform those that merely focus on economics and financial profits.[2]

Dellner epitomizes a new generation of investment bankers with a focus on creating a new generation of investment funds that invest in assets that yield a positive impact on the well-being of others. Dellner, the Swedish-born grandson of the founder of Saab Motors in Sweden, lives outside of London. When I met Robert he was the head of risk management at Assetz Capital, a new generation of peer-to-peer lending and investment banks based in London. Trained in psychology and finance, Robert understands the nature of risk as well as the nature of the human being.

In 2015 I visited Robert along with a number of other new investment banking colleagues to explore the creation of a new generation of impact investment funds and banks who would have a mission of doing the most possible good in the world, that would be oriented toward the well-being of our neighbors and creating a world in which we could become each other's bankers and invest more directly into the businesses and assets of our neighbors and our neighborhoods.

In those rich discussions in Robert's home, we acknowledged that the seductive power of money and the human tendency toward greed (which I believe is based on fear of lack) would be something that would be difficult to overcome. It was Robert who would later introduce me to Ken Costa through another London-based philanthropist Peter West (founder of The Bread Tin).

It seemed that in the heart of the world's money power (London), in people like Costa, Dellner, West, and Luke Eckblad (Boustead Asset LLC and Boustead and Co., the world's oldest merchant bank), I had found hope that the establishment of a new generation of investment banks and impact investment funds for well-being would not only be possible but would become the most important work of our lives. Of course, I realized that the journey would not be easy, fraught with challenges of egos, anxiety and opposition from others in the financial world who would view our efforts as a threat to their future. It would only be through a good dose of humility and grace that we could perceiver.

Robert Dellner now leads an important initiative within Lintel Capital LLC—a private equity fund and a new generation of impact investment funds that has been established on two core principles: a) the Hippocratic oath of "first, do no harm" and b) "that all investments are integral and aimed at doing as much good as possible." Robert and I have been working together on the development of new impact-investment protocols that bring together my model of integrated five-asset management for well-being and his understanding of risk and investment banking into a synthesis that we call integrated finance and accounting.

As Dellner notes, the key difference in today's world of finance is a growing awareness and consciousness amongst investment industry members that is shifting the previous monetary maximization paradigm toward measurable impacts and system outcomes. We are working on the development of the world's first integrated five-asset accounting model to guide the investment decisions of the Lintel investment portfolio that can measure and demonstrate to the investor families that their investments are contributing a net positive well-being impact and net positive well-being returns on their portfolio of investments.

Well-Being Impact Investment Funds

The development of a new generation of well-being impact investment financial models is one of the most promising ventures of my life. I am fortunate to be working with some of the most integral minds in the world of finance around the world, including Robert Dellner, Ronnie Lessem (DaVinci Institute, South Africa), Luke Eckblad (Boustead Asset Management LLC in Los Angeles), Alfred Jordan (Washington, D.C.) and Peter West (The Bread Tin) along with many others scattered throughout the world.

Robert and I have committed our lives to developing a practical model for impact-investment-fund management that would put well-being impacts and five-asset optimization at the heart of fund management. Lintel's fund management structure is based on the concept of integral finance, which is similar to my proposed integrated five-assets model described in previous chapters. Robert and I are in the process of testing integral finance and economic analytic protocols within Lintel's portfolio of investments. We are drawing from numerous sources for the development of a well-being impact investment fund architecture, including the B-Corp certification standards.

Robert is using the Integral model of finance developed by Ronnie Lessem and Alexander Schieffer at the DaVinci Institute. This work is part of Dellner's PhD work with Dr. Ronnie Lessem and Dr. Alexander Schieffer of the da Vinci Institute on the development of an integral model (Trans4M, trans-4-m.com) for finance and economics. I am serving as an external adviser to Dellner's PhD work and contributing to the development of integral accounting and impact investment analysis protocols that would support this financial institution's operations and decision-making.

The integral model (Figure 37) is based on the concept of "integral" which means the dynamic, integrated conclusion of all dimensions (including natural ones) of a human system (individual, organizational, communal or societal). There are four core dimensions of the integral economy: south (nature and community), east (culture and spirituality), north (science, systems, and technology) and west (finance and enterprise). Lessem and Schieffer argue that all four dimensions are held together by what they term a "moral code," an expression of innermost values that, if integrated in harmony, will lead to systems flourishing. This is similar to the four aspects of the Indigenous medicine wheel, directed by volition and a core set of individual and shared values. The Trans4M model is similar and complementary to the integrated

37   **The Integral Economy Model**

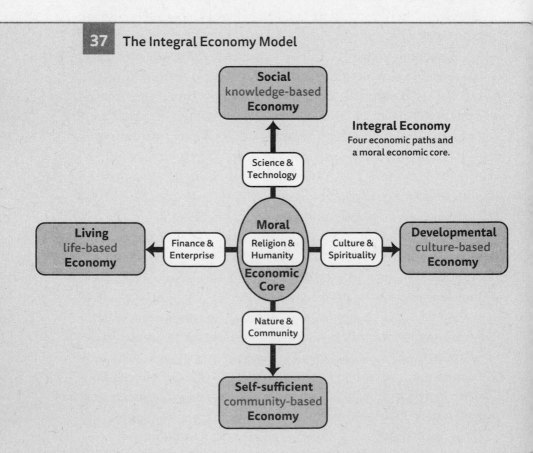

SOURCE: Lessem R and Schieffer A (2010). *Integral Economics: Releasing the Economic Genius of Your Society.* Abingdon, UK: Routledge.

five-asset model of a well-being economy, where all five assets of a community or nation are in harmony held together by a moral core of values.

This will require a nomenclature and structure of accounts and accounting protocols (as laid out in the previous chapters) that would guide all decisions, based on the notion that well-being impacts from a variety of forms of capital assets can be accounted for and measured in quantitative, qualitative, and monetary terms. We are in the early stages of developing such a system and testing it. To the extent that the well-being-impact investment system is successful for shaping Lintel Capital's investment decisions, it could become a model for future investment fund management and investment/merchant banking, beginning in London and extending to other parts of the world.

Indeed, it would be fitting that this new generation of impact investment finance would originate from the City of London—a corporation founded as part of the Magna Carta more than eight hundred years ago, the heart of the world's banking power and the birthplace of Bank of England (est. 1694), the world's second central bank after Sweden.

And the Times, They are a-Changin'

Movies like *Wall Street* (1986), *Jerry McGuire* (1996), *The Wolf of Wall Street* (2013) and *The Big Short* (2015) epitomize the culture of money and the money power that is associated with the financial world of Wall Street and London's financial district. They depict a world of insatiable greed, fear and lack of any moral ethic or concern for the well-being of others. What *The Big Short* taught me was that the world of finance, banking and investment, is in part the creation of our imagination. The person portrayed in the *The Big Short*, Michael Burry (Scion Capital), gave me hope for the future. Michael, against all odds, bet against the biggest investment banks realizing that a number of subprime home loans were in danger of defaulting. Burry did what others caught up in the frenzy of market frenzy did not; he looked into the very integrity

"Show me the money!"
—Tom Cruise in
Jerry McGuire, 1996

of each home mortgage and the risk to those subprime households. He understood how to examine the integrity and resilience
of an asset: homes. He understood that banking and financial
loans were not based on the underlying real value and utility of
an asset (the home) but the financial health of the household and
their ability to service the mortgage loan. Burry seemed to understand that investing in real verifiable assets, not phantom wealth,
is the path to financial resiliency. He is now focused on investing
in water (water rights, water-rich farmland, water utilities and
infrastructure) based on his belief that water and water-related
businesses will play a more and more critical role in the future of
this world.[3] This includes the intangible well-being benefits that
come from healthy watersheds that provide clean water and life
needs, at no cost.

Whether Michael Burry represents a new generation of
impact-investment finance is debatable. There are, however, signs
that the financial world is more receptive to the idea of well-being-
impact investment According to January 27, 2015 column, in *The
New York Times* by columnist David Brooks, a new era is dawning
in the investment world, which has been termed "impact investing." According to Brooks, "Impact investors seek out companies
that are intentionally designed both to make a profit and provide
a measurable and accountable social good. Impact funds are fre-
quently willing to accept lower financial returns for the sake of
doing good—say a 7 percent annual return compared with an 11
percent return."

I believe there is an increasing number of investors, like my-
self, who are interested in investing their after-tax dollars in investments that will generate a reasonable financial return while
also contributing to a net positive impact on the well-being of
the community in which a business operates and on the environment. For example, in my own investment experience, I find it remarkable that there are literally no financial investment advisers
who can help me invest directly in the equity or debt of a local
business even though I spend after-tax money on the purchase of
local goods and services. When I ask investment advisers for local

investment opportunities, they look puzzled and defer my question to their investment advisers in Toronto. What if we could align our investment choices with our local purchasing choices? I believe there is an opportunity for a new generation of local banks and investment funds that would facilitate the financing of both equity and debt in neighborhood-based enterprises and community assets.

A new generation of business students and financial professionals will be required to build this new financial architecture that is oriented toward an ethic of "doing well by doing good" and helping you and me contribute to the well-being of our communities with every dollar we make, spend and invest. Is it possible that a new generation of financial capitalism is emerging that can transcend a culture of greed and fear that has predominated in the world for centuries?

Notes

1. godatwork.org.uk/person/ken-costa.
2. lintelcapital.com/philosophy/. Accesssed June 2, 2017
3. valuewalk.com/2016/02/michael-burry-water/. Accessed December 8, 2017.

CHAPTER 9

The Community Asset
Well-Being Fund

IN MAY OF 2015 I was invited by Peter Block (co-author of *The Abundant Community: Awakening the Power of Families and Neighborhoods*, with John McKnight) to help inspire a conversation about the future of money and banking as part of a multi-faith community conversation in Cincinnati. The initiative is called the Economics of Compassion and is mentored by Walter Brueggermann (Old Testament scholar), John McKnight and many others.

Spending time with such remarkable elders and mentors is a humbling experience. What could I possibly teach these men and women about money and finance that would align with their aspiration for an economy of compassion?!

Peter Block had asked me to share my ideas for the creation of a new system of banking and finance to address some of the most pressing issues facing cities like Cincinnati, including systemic poverty, lack of affordable housing, crushing personal debt levels, lack of living wages and the struggling economy in the rust-belt economies of the central US states.

I proposed a new financial architecture in which members of church communities and the neighborhoods could become each other's bankers, support each other through mutual exchange, and create cooperative business enterprises and a new generation of community asset development funds. This would all be done on the basis of the principles of the highest and best use of community assets, including undervalued personal skills, gifts, talents and aspirations that would make up an economic ecosystem of reciprocity and sharing in the abundant assets resident in the neighborhood.

I explained how banks create the majority of money when they issue loans as book-keeping entries that are not actually backed by the assets of the household or the community. That these loans carry with them the crushing burden of interest costs that are found hidden in the costs of all goods and services. That the poorest households suffer disproportionately more than the wealthy ones, paying a much higher percentage of their incomes on interest costs of total societal debts, which are disproportionately held the top 5% of households in the community. The transfer of financial power to the wealthiest households occurs very slowly over time; after more than 60 years of this wealth transfer since WWII, we now have the conditions of massive wealth inequity in the United States. I explained how the vast majority of investment dollars invested in church endowments or trusts, community foundation investment funds and private retirement investment funds never contribute to building of Cincinnati's assets, including affordable housing for the poor, aspiring entrepreneurs and local businesses, sustainable food systems, renewable energy capacity and other undercapitalized local assets.

I began to sketch out a new architecture for well-being-based banking, investment and finance, where the money needed to build community assets in Cincinnati would come from each other's investment portfolios. We spoke about the creation of a new well-being fund for Cincinnati that would invest in community assets and a new public bank or credit union that would operate without charging interest on loans.

Initially we developed the Jubilee Fund concept. We used the term Jubilee in reference to another initiative, the Jubilee Housing Project, that had arisen out of the ECI conversations. The Jubilee Housing Project was led by Rev. Thomas Hargis, a Methodist minister whose church and ministry was to secure affordable housing for the poorest households in the most distressed neighborhoods in Cincinnati, restoring heritage homes (now boarded up) financed with interest-free mortgages and employing men and women who struggled to find work (halfway house men out of prison) and African-American youth. What I saw in the Hargis's model was the potential to eliminate poverty by reducing the cost of housing for the poor, build real home equity and eliminate the burden of interest on the lowest-income households in Cincinnati. I would later discover that the Edmonton, Alberta, Habitat for Humanity model for affordable housing has virtually the same features as the Jubilee Housing Project developed by Rev. Hargis, providing zero-interest home equity mortgages for low-income households in Edmonton.

Hargis's Jubilee Housing Project inspired me to pursue the development of a special-purposed community asset development fund that I called the Well-Being Fund for Cincinnati. I spoke to some of the most influential people in Cincinnati, including wealthy church foundation trusts, various church leaders, the mayor of Cincinnati, the city's chief solicitor, the Cincinnati Community Foundation, other nonprofit organizations, Peter Block and others about launching a new well-being fund with seed dollars from existing local investment portfolios. I calculated that between $500,000 and $1 million investment in the Fund would be sufficient to create a self-sustaining fund to support Hargis's affordable housing enterprise.

The benefits and the well-being return on investments would be clear and measurable. They would include

+ Reduced cost of living for the poorest households by eliminating the high cost of interest paid through a normal home mortgage.
+ The benefits of reducing the cost of interest normally embedded in housing costs (whether a mortgage or rent) would be the equivalent of paying a low-income household a living wage.
+ Mortgage payments would be based on a percentage of household income, never exceeding 25% of pre-tax household income, therefore meeting the affordable housing cost threshold of 30% of income.

- All mortgage payments made by the family or household would go into the Fund, building up equity that could be leveraged in the future.
- A typical low-income household would pay roughly $500 per month in their interest-free mortgage and could be debt free within 10 years or less. Being mortgage free and with considerably more disposable income so early in the life of a family would mean that the family could invest in other sustainable livelihood assets, send their kids to college or university with a zero-interest student loan and finance their retirement income based on the appreciating value of the equity in their home that resides in the Well-Being Fund.
- Building long-lasting home equity into a home for poor households in poor neighborhoods through interest-free mortgage payments into the new Fund, where the homes and property reside safe in the Fund, providing future collateral assets for future zero-interest lines of credit and retirement income.
- Eliminating the need for subsidized social and affordable rental housing throughout Cincinnati. This would save poor households thousands of dollars in rent payments and increase their disposable incomes enormously.
- Creation of new employment and skill development for construction trades for Cincinnati and all of Ohio.
- Reduction in the societal cost of poverty to the City of Cincinnati and the State of Ohio (based on estimates of the average societal cost of a person living in poverty at $30,000 per annum).

The Well-Being Fund would help alleviate the impact of poverty and unemployment as well as underemployment. Undervalued community assets would be identified and assessed along lines outlined in the asset valuation and verification section of this book. Existing trusts and local funds, including the Christ Church (Episcopal) Cathedral endowment fund (where the Proctor and Gamble families attended), would be invited to invest a portion of their endowments or trusts into this new Well-Being Fund. Initial capital investments would be in affordable housing development along the lines of Habitat for Humanity.

My preliminary economic and well-being impact analysis showed tremendous benefits to low-income households, who would save thousands of dollars in interest charges on a conventional mortgage while building real assets and equity in their home. The financial projections looked great. All we needed was the commitment of several church foundations or trusts, the blessing of Cincinnati's mayor and, potentially, investment dollars from the Cincinnati Community Foundation to develop full pro-forma for the Fund with the goal of launching the Fund within 12 months.

The Fund would be the first of its kind in North America; a model of community asset impact investment. Similar to a community fund that many cities have, this well-being fund will invest in neighborhood assets, including skills, capacities, competencies and other personal household and community assets that are currently being underutilized, resulting in conditions of poverty and lack of hope. The goal of the Well-Being Fund is to ensure the "highest and best use" and optimum well-being returns to the assets held within the Fund. The assets include the human, social and built (homes) assets of the neighborhood.

Other options for the use of the Well-Being Fund would be

1. **Interest-free micro enterprise loans.** The Well-Being Fund would make available start-up funding, possible zero-interest loans, to new business enterprises that could capitalize on underutilized or undervalued yet verified neighborhood assets. The Fund would work with the entrepreneurs to develop robust business plans and feasibility studies that could demonstrate a net positive well-being return on investment capital. This due diligence would provide assurance to the Fund managers and local investors and protect the financial viability of the business owners. Zero-interest financing would adopt the best practices of the JAK Members Bank in Sweden, an interest-free cooperative bank that provides small

interest-free loans to its members for home or small business needs. In addition the creation of a public bank for Cincinnati, similar to the Bank of North Dakota, would be explored to provide zero-interest, at-cost financing to local enterprises.

2. **Repayment of the debts of the poor.** The Fund could provide liquidity for debt retirement (e.g., high-interest pay-day and other such loans, credit card balances, etc.) for the poor in Cincinnati neighborhoods that would be in combination with financial literacy coaching. This would tie financial help to the goal of gaining control of their economic lives.

3. **Advocacy.** The Fund could become an advocate, a lobbyist for change in predatory practices, wage and debt slavery, usury, targeting local firms who are most deceptive and advertising.

4. **Education and Research.** Education and research to support the flourishing of the Well-Being Fund and Well-Being Forums into the future.

The Well-Being Fund would be managed with very strict well-being impact investment management protocols. The Fund managers would be informed by an inventory and fair valuation of community assets, whether those are housing, land, people, renewable energy opportunities, prospective business enterprises, social networks or relational capital. An inventory and valuation of community assets would be conducted through a well-being lens. Both tangible and intangible assets would be identified with fair market and potential economic well-being impact valuations. In addition, a thorough assessment of risk would be conducted. After all, the goal was to help ensure investments in assets that would yield long-term well-being benefits and flourishing as well as resilient neighborhoods.

As I worked on the architecture of this new Well-Being Fund, I became more excited that a new generation of well-being finance and investment was within our grasp to help solve some of the most long-standing issues of our time including poverty. All it would take is the collective will power of a few important leaders in the community to cut checks to launch the Fund.

So what has happened to the vision of this fund for Cincinnati? Sadly, without the strength of a local champion, the proposed fund in Cincinnati appears to have stalled. Perhaps it's because I live too far away in Canada to move the project forward. Perhaps it is a matter of conflicting visions for Cincinnati and the natural human condition, where it is easier to maintain the status quo and protect existing investment funds. Some may feel threatened by this new fund proposal or view the execution risk as too high.

Notwithstanding these reasons, the architecture of the Well-Being Fund and its proposed operations is a model that is transferrable to any other community or city in the US, Canada and the world. It is simply a matter of time until new ideas for building banks and investment funds that serve the common well-being aspirations of communities are put forward.

Eliminating Poverty in Cincinnati within a Generation

The most compelling potential benefits of the Well-Being Fund would be the elimination of poverty in Cincinnati within one or two generations. How? By reducing the cost of housing, which typically consumes 30–60% of the incomes of the poorest, low-income households in society.

Statistics for Cincinnati show that an estimated 21.5% of Cincinnati residents live below the poverty lined, defined as $22,500 for a family of four. I've calculated that nearly 40% of households earn less than $25,000 (roughly a living household wage) and 45% of households earn less than $40,000 per annum. I've estimated that 75,000 households in Cincinnati are living below a living-wage.

About 41.5% of Cincinnati households (55,023 households of 132,600 total households) are paying more than 30% of their income on housing/rent, which by definition places them in affordable housing conditions.

The Jubilee Housing Project guarantees that a typical household earning $24,000 or less will pay less than 25% of their income on housing with an interest-free mortgage through the Well-Being Fund. For example, an average Jubilee Housing

Project home valued at a replacement cost of $70,000 (the property/home was purchased for $1000 plus $35,000 in renovation costs) would cost the homeowner roughly $500 per month in principal-only payments. The mortgage would be paid off in roughly 10 years. Such a mortgage payment (without the costly burden of interest) is financially viable for a household earning $24,000, which would translate into an average hourly household wage of roughly $14/hour. (A living wage per person in Cincinnati is currently $9.27/hour.)

The economic benefits to the average household participating in the interest-free financial benefits of the Well-Being Fund and the Jubilee Housing Project are considerable. For example, a Well-Being mortgage on a $70,000-valued restored home in Cincinnati (about 52% of the average price of a Cincinnati home at $133,800) would mean a low-income young couple (25 years of age) both working at living wage of $9.27/hour (the estimated living wage for Cincinnati) would have a combined household income of $38,567 in Cincinnati. With mortgage payments of $500 per month, or $6,000 per year, the cost of shelter for this couple would only be 15.6% of a household living wage income, which is more affordable than any other low-income household in America.

The benefits to low-income households of living their entire life free of the burden of interest charges is considerable. As previously noted, the average American household with an average household income of $56,500 (2015 figures) will spend $33,233, or roughly $0.53 of every $1.00 of median household income, on interest charges that are currently embedded and hidden to all household, business and government outstanding debts of the United States (in excess of $65 trillion as of first quarter of 2017).[1]

The purpose of the Well-Being Fund would be to begin to alleviate the interest cost burden on households in Cincinnati, beginning with housing/mortgage debt. The typical couple living in a Jubilee Housing Project home would be debt-free within 11 years of home ownership.

The average American household will spend $10,000 per year, or over 20% of household expenditures, on shelter, whether in the form of mortgage payments (including interest costs) or rent. The average American family spends roughly $6,000 on food per annum, including eating at home and restaurant meals

By contrast, the annual costs of shelter for a Jubilee Housing Project household would be only $6,000 per year ($500 per month) for a much shorter period: 10 or 11 years only.

A 25-year-old married couple with children could find themselves with a significantly more disposable income ($6,000 per year more) by the time they reached 35 years of age.

Once the principal of the mortgage is paid in full, the house and property would be retained within the fund and booked at both market value and replacement cost value. This would provide future benefit to the homeowner and their children. Instead of the homeowner going to their regular commercial bank for a line of credit against the asset value of their home they could apply to the Well-Being Fund for a zero-interest line of credit for new credit financing, such as a vehicle, home renovations, or college loan for their children. The value of the homes of assets in the Well-Being Fund can become the basis of collateralized capital development, raising funds in the other parts of financial markets just as is done currently by investment and merchant banks

Both the homeowner and the equity investor in the Well-Being Fund would have the option, after paying off their mortgage in ten years, to retain their home and property as an asset in the Well-Being Fund. The asset could be held in the form of shares tied to the fair market valuation of their home and property. The property would appreciate inside the fund based on adjustments in fair market valuation. Moreover, the fund would also be invested in other assets in Cincinnati that may include renewable energy, local food systems, local businesses, etc., each generating its own returns on investment.

The assets in the fund also constitute collateral grade assets that can be leveraged to provide future credit that can benefit the same family or other households and assets in the neighborhood. For example, the fund units could be used to provide zero-interest loans for college or university education for the children of these families. Moreover, the home as asset could provide the collateral to generate an annuity income stream for retirement, yielding a sustainable living retirement income. Of course, the value of their main asset, their home, will be protected and even appreciate in value over time as property values increase. Even if property values stay constant with a constant quality of living, the fund is still able to pay a living wage backed by the home and property as an asset held by the fund.

The Well-Being Fund represents a vision for new financial architecture that will support local economic development and help to eliminate poverty, one of the most unresolved social issues of our time. Millions of dollars currently spent on trying to solve the poverty challenge would be saved. More importantly the psychic well-being and hope of millions of low-income households who are stuck in poverty would result in enormous societal savings, eliminating or reducing the need for social programs, subsidies, food stamps, subsidized rental housing and income supports. The cost of poverty to society is considerable; an estimated $30,000 per poor person per year in the province of Alberta. Saving on health care, policing, prisons and other costs associated with poverty would save considerable public sector spending on the poor. The well-being returns on investment would be clear: happier and more hopeful communities and the elimination of poverty within a single generation.

Notes

1. As noted, there is no official accounting of the actual cost of interest being paid on the total outstanding debts of the United States or any nation. Using estimates of average costs of household, consumer, business and government (public sector) debt, I've calculated an average of $6,636 interest payments per household for household/consumer debt ($12.2 trillion total outstanding), $6,916 interest payments per household for each household's portion of US Federal debt ($19.794 trillion) and $16,678 interest payments per US household associated with business, financial industry and foreign debt ($33.0 trillion).

CHAPTER 10

Banking on Well-Being

All Roads Lead to London: The Queen's Banker's Wife

In order to understand the origins of money and banking, one must journey to the heart of the world's financial power: the City of London Corporation. London, the Corporation, is the birthplace of modern banking and the world's second central bank, the Bank of England. It was in London in the late 17th century, that debt-based money and banking systems evolved.

I was invited to visit London, England, in the fall of 2014 to join a group of merchant or investment bankers and financiers who were motivated by a new consciousness of money and banking. Peter West, the founder of a philanthropic organization called The Bread Tin, invited me to attend a special event he was hosting at the House of Lords on the River Thames with the wife of the Queen's banker, Lady Penny Money Coutts. Yes, that's correct— her name actually contains the name Money and Penny!

The Corporation of London was established over 800 years ago as part of the signing of the Magna Carta in 1216, a site of a former Roman settlement known as Londinium abandoned by the Romans about AD 400. The crest of the Corporation of London is a double-breasted dragon.

London is the central investment banking power of Europe if not the world, with more commercial and merchant/investment bank offices than New York City. As Mark Carney, Bank of England governor (formally from Edmonton, Alberta, and former Bank of Canada governor) has noted, "The UK is effectively the investment banker for Europe. More than half the equity and debt raised (for

European governments and business) is raised in the UK, quite often from investors based in the United Kingdom."[1]

At the House of Lords I engaged in a fascinating discussion with several young entrepreneurs and business leaders about their knowledge of banking and money. We spoke about the ethics of business and of corporate social responsibility. I suggested that well-being might become a new business and finance ethic in heart of London's financial district.

The next day Peter West and I visited the Bank of England museum as well as the Rev. David Parrott, the rector of the St. Lawrence Jewry, the official church of the Crown Corporation of London. Rev. Parrott described his unique role as pastor in the Crown Corporation, providing a safe place for spiritual reflection, prayer and possibly moral and ethical guidance to some of the 300,000 bankers, insurance, other financial industry people who work there daily.

The Crown Corporation of London (like the Vatican) is actually a private state established over 800 years ago under the Magna Carta (1215). It is located in the heart of Greater London and has its own laws and its own Lord Mayor. The Corporation became a sovereign-state in 1694 when King William III of Orange privatised the Bank of England. The Crown in London houses the Bank of England, Lloyd's of London, the London Stock Exchange, and all British banks. It also houses the branch offices of 385 foreign banks, 70 US banks, as well as Fleet Street newspapers and publishing monopolies.

After meeting with Rev. Parrott, Peter West took me to visit the Bank of England Museum. I was curious to see if the museum had an artifact of the oldest form of money in England, the tally stick. Dating back to the founding of England under William the Conqueror in the 11th century, this notched wooden oak stick was the only source of money for more than eight hundred years in England. It was issued by the king and the king's treasurer in sufficient supply to meet the needs of the nation. This ingenious form of money ensured that Britain maintained economic stability with virtually no inflation for centuries. This stable financial epoch stands in stark contrast to today's unsustainable debt-based money systems that are all close to imminent collapse.

The tally stick system was eventually phased out, beginning with the founding of the Bank of England in 1694 under King William of Orange of Amsterdam.

The Bank of England was the first privately owned bank in the world that issued debt-money that was necessary to finance England's war efforts. The Bank of England has been the model for all central banks around the world, including the US Federal Reserve and the Bank of Canada.

I was struck by the similarity between the British tally stick and the Indigenous wampum belt sea-shell money systems that were in use for centuries across the Polynesian cultures of the Pacific and in North America.

What if a new money system could be adopted that was again directly linked to real natural assets such as land, trees and seashells? How would it operate? What if the creation of money were tied directly to the real assets of nations and the goal of maintaining the health and resiliency of ecosystems and watersheds for human flourishing?

Moreover, could money creation and the operations of other financial institutions (trusts, investment funds, community foundations, insurance companies) operate based on creating money in parallel with improving well-being in society?

I imagined a new era in banking and finance emerging from London itself and spreading to other financial capitals of New York, Hong Kong/Shanghai, Toronto and Frankfurt.

Freeing Economies of the Burden of Interest from Debt-Based Money

As noted in Chapter 2, the burden of compound interest on everyone in an economy is staggering. Freeing up the human energy, time and resources currently dedicated to paying interest costs on ever-rising private and public debts would unleash significant amounts of human potential, reduce the hours need to work for life's needs and alleviate the unnecessary carbon footprint on the environment. But the key question is, who should create money without the need to charge interest on its creation?

Most people assume that it is the central bank that creates the majority of money in our economy in the form of paper, plastic or other forms of currency. That is not true. The truth is that approximately 98% of our modern money is created by private banks when they create loans for our homes, cars, education and even for financing of government services. The Bank of England has now publicly confirmed that private banking institutions create more than 97% of all modern money in our economy through the practice of issuing loans. In fact, only a small fraction of what we call money is the form of government-created currency or notes.[2]

The idea that we "make money" is clearly untrue. All money is created as debt by banks.

The Bank of England states clearly how money is created in one of its new publications titled *Money Creation in the Modern Economy*:

> In the modern economy, most money takes the form of bank deposits. But how those bank deposits are created is often misunderstood: the principal way is through commercial banks making loans. Whenever a bank makes a loan, it simultaneously creates a matching deposit in the borrower's bank account, thereby creating new money. Commercial banks create money, in the form of bank deposits, by making new loans. When a bank makes a loan, for example to someone taking out a mortgage to buy a house, it does not typically do so by giving them thousands of pounds' worth of banknotes. Instead, it credits their bank account with a bank deposit of the size of the mortgage. At that moment, new money is created. For this reason, some economists have referred to bank deposits as "fountain pen money," created at the stroke of bankers' pens when they approve loans.[3]

The other truth is that money created by private corporations called banks do not lend against the inherent value of the assets that these loans are helping to finance. What matters to the bank issuing you a mortgage is not in fact the market value of your home but rather your ability to repay the principal and interest on the loan, in other words having a steady income.

Banks justify charging interest to cover their risk with borrowers and to cover operating costs. However, so long as banks (particularly public banks) recover their operating costs plus an allowance for the risk of loan defaults and a profit margin (unnecessary with a public bank), they should be satisfied to operate with these full costs recovered with a loan fee. Consider that since, by their own admission, banks create new money out of thin air each time they issue a loan with a simple ledger or bookkeeping entry, then what is the real cost of creating money or issuing loans?

Another mystery is the source of funds necessary to pay for the interest on each loan. Logically, since banks create all of our modern money as debt, then the new money needed to pay the compounding interest costs on loans must ultimately come from issuing new loans, which creates new liquidity. The result is a vicious upward spiral of compounding interest on exponentially rising levels of debt.

Can money be created without debt instruments? Could money be created as a public utility, at cost?

In principle, governments have the power to create all of the money needed to make an economy function and provide necessary, liquidity to investing in the full potential of a nation's or region's assets or wealth. In theory, new money can be issued as a public service for the well-being of all at a fraction of the cost currently imposed by interest charges.

Take, for example, Canada. Prior to 1973 the Bank of Canada was empowered to create enough credit for the benefit of the Government of Canada to provide goods and services to all Canadians. Under the leadership of Prime Minister Pierre Trudeau in 1974, the power of money creation was transferred to private banks, who took over the role of money creation. This came ultimately at a high cost to all Canadians. Canada's public sector debt remained remarkably stable over a long period, from World War I through to the late 1950s. In 1972 it stood at $28 billion. Because Canada could create its own debt-money at virtually no cost, the total debt remained extremely stable and relatively low compared with GDP. However, with the federal government handing over power of public debt creation to private banks, Canada's debt has grown dramatically, reaching over $1.1 trillion in outstanding federal debt in 2016 (total national debt without netting out the value of financial assets).[4] The estimated annual interest on this national debt in 2017 was expected to be $27.7 billion. In 2015–16 such interest charges represented 8.6% of Canada's total federal government program expenditures—higher than unemployment insurance payments ($19.4 billion) or children's benefits ($18.0 billion).[5,6]

What is remarkable is that this national debt is held primarily by private commercial banks and other investors, which would be unnecessary if the Bank of Canada had maintained the public banking powers it had before 1973. Moreover, the interest charges paid on the debt are an unnecessary drain on all Canadians. While federal public debt charges to federal revenues have been declining since 1992, the burden on Canadians remains significant—and mostly unnecessary.

If Canada were to return to an era of public debt money creation as it was prior to 1973, it could direct the Bank of Canada to issue zero-interest financing to fund the programs, services and capital investments (e.g., infrastructure renewal) of the Government of Canada, savings millions of taxpayer dollars. The same is true for the US, though the US Federal Reserve remains a privately-owned central banking conglomerate.

A Public Bank for Well-Being

In addition to national public banks, the creation of state, provincial and municipal public banks could also serve to alleviate the unnecessary burden of interest costs in the economy. This does not mean putting commercial and investment banks out of business. Rather this would entail chartering and reconstituting existing financial institutions with a financial well-being mandate to serve best interests of the well-being economy.

What is a Public Bank and Could It Be Structured to Support the Economy of Well-being?

There are many types of banks, including commercial banks (e.g., Bank of America, TD Financial), credit unions and public banks. The word *bank* originated in the Renaissance and comes from the Italian word *banco*, which means "bench" or "desk." The general role of commercial banks is to provide financial services to the general public and businesses, ensuring economic and social stability and sustainable growth of the economy. The provision of "credit creation" through loans is the most significant function of commercial banks. Commercial banks are either privately owned or are publicly traded shareholder-based corporations.

A public bank is a bank that is controlled and owned by public actors, namely the state or a government body rather than by private investors. Public banking is common around the world, particularly in developing and newly developed countries. Globally, about 40% of banks are publicly owned. The countries with public banks mostly survived the credit crisis of 2007.

According to the Public Banking Institute based in the United States,

> Public banking is distinguished from private banking in that its mandate begins with the public's interest. Privately-owned banks, by contrast, have shareholders who generally seek short-term profits as their highest priority. Public banks are able to reduce taxes within their jurisdictions, because their profits are returned to the general fund of the public entity. The costs of public projects undertaken by governmental bodies are also greatly reduced, because public banks do not need to charge interest to themselves. Eliminating interest has been shown to reduce the cost of such projects, on average, by 50%.[7]

A public bank is in essence an extension of the government that created it, whether that of a nation, a municipal government or a First Nation. In principle the government can borrow from its own public bank without having to pay interest charges. Because a public bank need not generate large profits to satisfy shareholder expectations, as with large nations and international commercial banks, the creation of credit and financial services can be more affordable for citizens. In other words, a public bank can be a source of low-cost credit to both government and the citizens of a state, province or nation. Public banks therefore have natural advantages.

Public banks can be prohibited from speculating in risky derivatives like commercial and investment banks do, which can't be adequately regulated. This would prevent bailouts that ultimately burden the taxpayer, as we saw with the 2007–08 global financial crisis, perhaps the worst financial crisis since the Great Depression. Further because of the fractional reserve banking system (which allows banks to lend multiple times more than deposits), public banks can magnify the money the government can deploy for economic development, infrastructure investment and other community assets, up to ten dollars or more of investment in loans for local interests from each dollar the governing entity sends to its public bank.

The Bank of North Dakota and ATB (Alberta Treasury Branch): The Most Important Public Banks in North America

The best-known public banks in North America are the Bank of North Dakota (BND, with US$7.5 billion in assets),[8] founded in 1919, and the Alberta Treasury Branch (ATB Financial, with C$46.7 billion in assets),[9] founded in 1938. Public banking was first introduced in the US by the Quakers in the original colony of Pennsylvania. Other colonial governments also established publicly owned banks. The concept was later embraced by the State of North Dakota, the only state to currently own its own bank.

In 2016 the BND had assets of $6,870 million, loans of $4,790 million and equity of $875.7 million.[10] It had very low operating

38	Comparing ATB Financial, Servus Credit Union Financial and Bank of North Dakota

	ATB Financial	Servus	Bank of North Dakota
Loans ($ millions)	40,811	13,109	4,790
Operating Costs ($ millions)	1,044.4	307.6	31.0
Provision of Loan Losses (% of loans)	1.25%	0.24%	0.33%

SOURCE: ATB Financial 2017 Annual Report; Bank of North Dakota Annual Report 2016; Servus Credit Union Consolidated Financial Statements for the year ended October 31, 2016.

costs of only $31 million, or a mere 0.65% of total loan portfolio value. BND's provision for loan losses was $16 million, or only 0.33% of total loans. That means that the combined cost of money plus allowance for risk/losses was less than 1% of the value of money created in the form of loans. Therefore, BND is the most competitive public bank in North American that I have analyzed. (See Figure 38, which compares ATB Financial with BND and Servus, Alberta's largest credit union.)

Both BND and ATB Financial were founded to provide a dependable supply of affordable credit for all Albertans: farmers, ranchers, businesses and households. Today BND makes low interest loans to students, existing small businesses and start-ups. It partners with private banks to provide a secondary market for mortgages and supports local governments by buying municipal bonds.

ATB's financial services are more extensive, providing the same range of financial services as commercial banks, including mortgages, business loans, deposit accounts, credit card services and investment portfolio services.

The key benefit of having a state or provincial public bank is that it means all the state or provincial assets are used to capitalize

BND and ATB Financial. In theory, both public banks could generate enough loans to support the full potential of the state's or province's human, social, natural and built assets.

In the case of BND, all state revenues are deposited in the bank, by law.

ATB operates slightly differently than BND, providing a broader suite of financial services to Albertans than BND, with full deposit account and credit services to Albertans and businesses. Moreover, ATB pays no taxes and does not have to generate a profit, though it regularly pays a small dividend from net earnings to the provincial government. BND also pays a dividend to its only shareholder—the people of North Dakota. In the past decade, despite the state's small population and modest volume of economic activity, the Bank of North Dakota has returned over $300 million to the state's general fund, helping to ensure regular annual surpluses and eliminate the need for drastic tax increases or spending cuts for vital public services.

Public banks could in principle be chartered and managed so they deliver well-being benefits through lending against the assets within the jurisdiction in which they operate. The extent to which the legal mandate or act that governs a public bank is expressed in terms of the "well-being-best-interests of citizens" signals a new generation of public banking. Therefore a public bank like ATB can invest directly through loans to maximize the public good within the province by investing directly in the real potential of the province's full suite of human, social, built and natural capital assets, which are likely in trillions of unaccounted dollars. Maximizing well-being return on investment in provincial assets would trump maximizing profits through global investment strategies of commercial banks.

Alberta Treasury Branch: North America's Best Kept Secret

ATB Financial is undoubtedly one of the largest and most successful public banks in the world, given Alberta's population. What does it mean to have our own public bank? How could the natural advantages of a public bank like ATB Financial help build a new economy of well-being for Alberta and be a model for the rest of North America and the world?

The Alberta Treasury Branch (ATB) was established in 1938 in the midst of the depression to serve the credit needs of all Albertans. Today ATB Financial has become one Alberta's most exceptional modern financial institutions—essentially a public bank.

ATB's story is unique in the history of banking. Establishing Alberta-run "credit houses" was the brainchild of William Aberhart, Alberta's first Social Credit premier, who created the Alberta Treasury Branches (ATB Financial predecessors) to meet the financial crisis brought about by the Great Depression. According to historian James G. Macgregor, the Alberta Treasury Branches were designed to unlock the riddle of what Premier Aberhart called "poverty in the midst of plenty." In the face of this devastating crisis and an unprecedented contraction of credit, the Alberta government decided 80 years ago to set up its own lending institution to have control over the curtailment or release of our own credit.

ATB Financial is now governed under the *Alberta Treasury Branches Act* of 2000, with a clear mandate of providing financial services to all Albertans as an arm of the Government of Alberta. It is not a chartered bank and, unlike all banks operating in Canada, is regulated entirely by a government—the Government of Alberta, under the authority of the *Alberta Treasury Branches Act*, RSA 2000, c. A-37, and Treasury Branches Regulation 187/97. ATB operates 172 branches and 135 agencies, serving 4.3 million Albertans in 243 communities across the province, headquartered in Edmonton with more than 5,300 employees. The legislation is modeled on the statutes and regulations governing other financial institutions and other guidelines to financial institutions issued by the federal Office of the Superintendent of Financial Institutions and the Canada Deposit Insurance Corporation. ATB Financial is one of 15 financial institutions that participate in Canada's Large Value Transfer System.

In 2017, ATB Financial had $47.135 billion in assets—$19.046 billion in business loans, $14.948 billion in residential mortgages,

$6.623 billion in personal loans and $704 million in credit card credit—serving 730,000 member account holders.[11] In terms of assets, ATB is currently almost seven times larger than BND—but Alberta's population (4,286,134)[12] is 5.6 times larger than North Dakota's (757,952).[13]

Ironically, unlike other public banks, which can legally provide loans to local or state governments, ATB Financial has not yet provided such a service to the Government of Alberta or to municipal governments of Alberta. However, ATB does provide direct lending to Alberta consumers and businesses. This service is otherwise restricted for public banks like BND, who are authorized by the state to make only low-interest-rate loans to students, which the state views as beneficial because it helps invest in human intellectual capital assets.

Another key advantage of having a public bank for creation of credit through loans is that in principle loans can be provided at cost of operating the bank and thus without a need to charge interest. For example, in 2016 ATB's operating costs were the equivalent of 2.5% of their $40.35 million in loans with a loan-loss allowance of $473 million representing 1.17% of total loans. By contrast, BND had operating costs of 0.65% of their $4.79 billion in loans and a loan-loss allowance of a mere 0.33%. This would suggest that BND could create loans/credit at less than 1.0% of loan values. ATB appears to have a much higher operating cost regime for reasons that are not entirely clear.

It is a significant revelation that public banks could create loans, credit or money for the well-being benefit of both citizens and the government without the need to charge interest on loans, but simply recover the operating costs plus an allowance for loan losses at less than 1.0%. Everyone would benefit from this system.

Why Could ATB Financial Become the Model for Public Well-Being Banks Across North America?

First, ATB Financial is not a private bank but a full-service public bank with full financial services that is owned by Albertans and backed 100% by the assets of the province. ATB Financial is so safe that the only way it could fail is if the entire province experienced a massive asset devaluation.

Second, ATB Financial is governed by a special Act of legislature called the Alberta Treasury Branches Act (2000) that sets out the terms of financial services ATB Financial can provide on behalf of the needs of Albertans. ATB Financial has the same special power of fractional reserve banking as any other private bank.

Third, ATB Financial has the legal powers to operate just like any other bank; however, being a public bank it has the potential to also provide government with credit, at cost (of operating) and without interest charges. ATB Financial could effectively serve as Alberta's public financial utility creating money and credit for Alberta households, business and even governments at below conventional banking rates and potentially at cost of creating and managing loans, without the need to charge interest on loans.

Fourth, ATB does not need to generate a profit to the government of Alberta since it exists as for the financial well-being benefits of all Albertans. Moreover, because it is a public institution it does not pay taxes; in lieu of taxes, ATB makes a small dividend payment to the Alberta Government. This is because ATB Financial is an asset of the Government of Alberta and is exempt from paying income taxes. No other bank in Canada has such benefits. ATB Financial is required to pay a levy in lieu of not paying taxes. For the three months ended June 30, 2016, ATB Financial paid the Government of Alberta a mere $7,466 in dividends in lieu of taxes.

Fifth, ATB Financial has one of the healthiest balance sheets of any bank in the world. Healthy bank balance sheets have strong equity-to-asset ratios. The assets of ATB Financial include loans to Albertans, which totaled more than $40.811 billion in 2017. Liabilities include the deposit accounts of Albertans, which totaled $33.928 billion, and $11.472 billion in other liabilities, including wholesale borrowing, collateralized borrowings and $156 million in derivative financial instruments (a mere 0.3% of ATB Financial assets, which is very small for a bank). The difference between assets and liabilities constitutes net equity, which in 2017 amounted to $3.147 billion, or a net equity-to-asset ratio of 2.6% (down from 7.2% in 2015). These are signs of a very healthy and vibrant bank.

How would interest-free public banking work? Since in principle banks operate like any other business, they have to recover their operating costs plus allow for the risk of loan losses (non-performing loans). Since ATB and BND are not required to generate a profit or pay taxes, they have a natural competitive operating cost advantage over commercial banks.

How much does it cost to create and manage new loans and credit at ATB? This all depends on the type of loan or credit the bank creates. For example, the exact cost of creating a new mortgage and managing the loan over the life of the mortgage would have to be determined. Whether these costs represent 1–3% of the total value of the home mortgage is unknown.

ATB Financial's statements for 2016–17 show that the cost of its operations as a ratio of total loans ($40.8 billion) was 2.56%. In addition, there was a loan-loss provision of $510 million, or 1.25% of total loans. Of course, not 100% of operating costs are attributed to loans; the exact allocation is not known.

Compared to the Bank of North Dakota, ATB has high operating costs and loan-loss provisions. In 2016 BND had operating costs that were as low as 0.6% of its US$4.3 billion loan portfolio and a loan loss provision of only 0.29% of its loan portfolio. Therefore, the BND is providing loans and other banking services for less than 1% of loans, a remarkably efficient operating cost.

This analysis illustrates the potential of public banks operating as efficiently as BND to provide money (credit) at less than 1% of the value of debt money created to invest in local and state/provincial assets in the well-being interests of citizens.

The benefits of using the full potential of ATB as Alberta's public bank are clear. Individual Albertans and Alberta businesses could save significantly from lower costs of credit and lower student loan rates, and save the Alberta Government millions in interest charges they may now be paying on private-bank debts they have assumed to cover Alberta's significant budget deficit. Whether the Alberta government understands the true potential of ATB Financial to serve the debt needs of the provincial government is a question. However, the potential benefits of a full service public bank are clear.

When I explain the true nature of ATB Financial to my colleagues in London, Washington, San Francisco, South Africa, the Netherlands and Nigeria, they are astounded. I imagine Alberta's public bank model being transferrable to any US or Canadian state, province or municipality.

I imagine ATB becoming the first prototype public well-being bank. New protocols for creating credit through at-cost loans tied to leveraging the full potential of verifiable assets across all five capital asset classes are possible. ATB Financial, like the Alberta Investment Management Corp with $95.7 billion under management,[14] would be accountable to the Alberta Treasury Board and the finance minister, accounting for the well-being impacts and well-being ROI of their lending and investment decisions. These decisions would be supported by a proper provincial total asset accounting system and balance sheet.

What kinds of well-being investments and financing are possible? Investments in a number of asset classes could include

+ Affordable housing, applying Edmonton's successful Habitat for Humanity interest-free home mortgage equity model.
+ Alberta's untapped and undercapitalized renewable energy potential, making Alberta a model of the green energy economy while reducing Alberta's massive unfunded carbon liability.
+ Interest-free loans to First Nations, Métis and Inuit people of Alberta to invest in building affordable sustainable housing, water treatment systems, better roads, Indigenous youth skills, Elder traditional knowledge and other cultural assets.

Alberta households would all benefit from interest-cost savings on their mortgages, student loans, farm loans, lines of credit and credit card debts. Creating money and credit based on the real utility and potential of a community's assets would be a key to building a flourishing and resilient economy of well-being.

Benjamin Frankin's Philadephia Experiment

In 1729, at the age of 23, Benjamin Franklin published a pamphlet in colonial Pennsylvania titled *A Modest Inquiry into the Nature and Necessity of a Paper Currency*. In it, he addressed three key monetary questions that are very seldom asked: What is money? Who should be entrusted to create money? And, what, if anything, should backstop money to support its value?

Ironically, these are the very questions going through the mind of Jon Matonis, secretary of the Bitcoin Foundation. Matonis and his associates are guardians of the complex computer algorithms that lie behind the Bitcoin, the revolutionary new digital currency. The value of Bitcoin soared from a mere US$0.30 in February 2011 to an astronomical high of US$19,167 on December 16, 2017, having since retreated to under US$7,000 per Bitcoin in February 2018.

In the early 18th century Franklin championed the idea of a "colonial" currency: paper money issued directly by colonial legislatures. He understood that a chronic shortage of gold and silver coins, the standard imperial currency, was harming the economy. When the Pennsylvania legislature starting issuing its own paper (fiat) money, it significantly increased the supply of money, which increased business volumes and helped end the recession, to the delight of the locals.

Franklin's answer to this problem of money shortages was unique for his time: backstop the colonial paper money supply with something real, not base metals but Pennsylvania's sturdiest asset, land. Why land? Because he realized that genuine money is derivative of real value that resides elsewhere, in a more primary source. For Franklin that primary source must be a solid asset that could be translated relatively easily into labor. He preferred land both because, unlike base metals, it was readily available in Pennsylvania and because it was more likely to hold its labor value than gold and silver coins.

The Future of Money: Well-Being Currency

I envision an economy in which money is returned to a virtuous role of serving the well-being needs of the people. A future where chartered banks have a legal mandate to serve the economic well-being needs and aspirations of communities. And where central, state, provincial and local banks are genuinely public banks, creating the necessary money supply needed to finance the full potential of the community's full array of assets.

This is a world that I believe was envisioned by Benjamin Franklin in the 1770s (with his Philadelphia experiment tying money to the productivity of land), Abraham Lincoln in the 1860s (with his greenback currency) and William Aberhart in Alberta in the 1930s (with the creation of North America's largest public bank, ATB Financial).

I envision a modern financial architecture that utilizes the best of cryptocurrencies and blockchain technologies that have spawned a plethora of digital money, including Bitcoin and the new Etherium. Blockchain technologies provide an ideal technology for aligning individual and community assets to money. A group of us interested in blockchain technologies are working on a new prototype model that would link individual assets to cryptocurrencies that could become part of a unique financial ecosystem that may replace the need for banks all together.

Bitcoin was created, in part, to redress a chronic shortage of money in key sectors of the modern economy. The Bitcoin is a cryptocurrency and digital payment system where transactions take place between users (peer to peer) verified by a network of nodes that are recorded in a public distribution system of ledgers called a blockchain. The blockchain is a public ledger that records every Bitcoin transaction; therefore all transactions between people are publicly transparent. Bitcoin is thus the world's first decentralized currency system created by computer algorithms. The Bitcoin was modeled, in part, after gold because of its inherent respected value (as a hedge or alternative to fiat or paper currencies) and its relative physical limits of supply.

I believe the explosion of interest in Bitcoin and other cryptocurrencies is a response to a shortage of real money, or money that is tied to real assets rather than simply bank-created debt money, ex nihilo bookkeeping entries.

Like Franklin's "colonial" currency, Bitcoin is providing the resources needed to accelerate growth in undercapitalized assets and sectors of the economy. However, if cryptocurrencies, co-created by individuals in communities, are going to become genuine money they will need to be designed to fulfill money's second role as a store of value. This means linking the cryptocurrency directly to real wealth and verifiable assets. I am yet to be convinced that Bitcoin and other cryptocurrencies will endure as an alternative to fiat debt money and a genuine democratization of money; however the democratization of money is a worthy aspiration. I have my doubts whether Bitcoin represents the democratization of money with its wild valuation swings and seemingly susceptible to less democratic forces since its inception. The problem is, uniting the two roles of money, as a medium of exchange and a store of value, is extremely difficult. However, with blockchain technologies this is now increasingly possible.

As such, there has rarely been a form of currency in our economic history that has accomplished the role as a genuine store of value that reflects the assets and well-being conditions of individuals and communities.

Like other modern forms of currency, Bitcoin is not a genuine store of value. Bitcoins are nothing more than digits or numbers that reside on the hard drives of those who are using it as a unit of exchange. The power of Bitcoin is as vulnerable as our current money (currency) in that its purchasing power can be wiped out by a crash of your hard drive or a loss in confidence in its purchasing power, such as we have just witnessed.

In Cincinnati, the Jubilee Project is exploring new cryptocurrency systems whereby individuals co-create digital money, let's call it the Jubilee, that uses the blockchain technology to store and transact individual, household and community assets (including skills, competencies, ideas, and other personal assets). The management of the Jubilee would be through the proposed Cincinnati

Well-Being Asset Fund. The Jubilee would be a local currency accepted throughout Cincinnati as both a store of value and payment system for goods, services and contracts amongst and between neighbors in Cincinnati neighborhoods. The Jubilee could become the first local cryptocurrency that could be used to pay a living wage to the estimated 75,000 households who currently live below a living wage in Cincinnati.

The Jubilee could be issued directly by the Well-Being Fund similarly to how private banks currently issue loans. However, the key difference is that new Jubilees would be issued in direct relationship with the asset potential of individuals, households and local businesses.

Unlike Bitcoin and other cryptocurrencies or local dollar initiatives, the Jubilee would be designed and managed with a singular goal in mind: to finance the highest and best use of the gifts, talents, skills and aspirations of individuals and households in neighborhoods, making the best of abundant and often idle community or neighborhood assets. The Jubilee would be accepted only in Cincinnati to facilitate the exchange of time, resources, talents, skills and competencies between and amongst neighbors through what is known as smart contracts, without the need for legally formalized contracts.[15] The exchange between peers on the blockchain would occur based on the level of trust developed between two or more individuals. The Jubilee would mean that each of us would become each other's banker, independent yet cooperative.

Through the actions of both the Well-Being Asset Fund and the Jubilee, it would become possible to eliminate poverty by ensuring that every Cincinnati person and household received a fair and living wage commensurate with their skills and assets. The Jubilee would be used to pay for affordable housing development, including successful projects like Habitat for Humanity and the Jubilee Housing Project. The result would be a resilient and flourishing economy modelled after a healthy forest ecosystem where Jubilees (money) are simply the currency that flows easily and fluidly throughout the city to facilitate healthy exchange of gifts to meet needs and achieve well-being outcomes. The Jubilee would provide each individual the freedom to make the highest and best use of their own talents, skills and competencies and pursue entrepreneurial ideas that make sound economic and business sense, while contributing to the overall well-being conditions of neighborhoods.

What distinguishes the Jubilee from other cryptocurrencies like Bitcoin is that money would be created by individuals based on their own unique set of assets. Each individual would be free to exchange their Jubilees with others in the community in order to meet their life needs. Individuals and households within neighborhoods (human ecosystems) could be empowered to create their personal asset portfolio and place it on a blockchain.

Every child born in the United States or Canada will have roughly 740,000 hours of life to live. Time is the most precious asset, with the potential to contribute to personal, community and societal well-being. Imagine a world where every person born has absolute sovereignty over their life energy (time), to trade and use it as they wish to contribute their best skills, talents and dreams to contribute to the overall well-being of the planet. Currently, that is not the case. Much of our time—particularly the hours we spend working for money—is literally mortgaged, committed to earning wages, about half of which are unwittingly going to pay the interest on the society's outstanding financial debts (mortgages, consumer credit, business loans and government debts). Imagine your life if you had genuine discretion and freedom over this extra available time to dedicate it to your dreams and aspirations for a better life and a better world.

Individual assets (including time and skills) could be structurally and legally incorporated as a human right for every individual in society, with a unique and distinct portfolio that would be immutable. Smart contracts would become the basis of exchange of personal assets, skills and competencies; smart contracts are self-enforced and self-executed. The aim of smart contracts is to provide security that is superior to traditional contract law and to reduce other transaction costs associated with contracting. No new assets could be created; only the Jubilee values of personal assets could be exchanged or transferred. A record of each trans-action and the terms of relationships amongst individuals in neighborhoods would be immutable.

The total supply of Jubilees could be determined by a board of well-being fund trustees using community well-being asset accounts at the city and the neighborhood level. From these ac-counts, the well-being conditions and needs would be assessed, thus identifying more (or sometimes less) Jubilees in the system. The primary mandate and goal of the fund would be improving the overall well-being for all people. The Jubilee would oper-ate within a zero-interest financial architecture (the Well-Being Fund and Well-Being Public Bank) so that all Cincinnati residents would eventually be free of the burden of interest costs in their economic lives. This would unleash pent-up human energy to contribute more discretionary time to building a Cincinnati econ-omy of well-being.

These projects are still at an early stage of development, but the architectural blueprint is already in place. As with all well-being economy initiatives, a shared commitment of time and energy will be required to build these new economies, but once we have built them, we will look back and wonder what took us so long.

Notes

1. Cited February 15, 2018 from *The Guardian*. theguardian.com/business /2016/nov/30/mark-carney-european-economies-face-hit-if-cut-off -from-city-of-london.
2. positivemoney.org/how-money-works/proof-that-banks-create -money/. Accessed June 2, 2017.
3. Money Creation in the Modern Economy available at bankofengland .co.uk/publications/Documents/quarterlybulletin/2014/qb14q1pre releasemoneycreation.pdf. Accessed June 2, 2017.
4. Based on the nationaldebtclocks.org statistics that are derived from the Government of Canada's debt figures. nationaldebtclocks.org/.
5. fin.gc.ca/afr-rfa/2016/report-rapport-eng.asp. Accessed May 16, 2017.
6. fin.gc.ca/afr-rfa/2016/report-rapport-eng.asp#_Toc463249479. Ac-cessed May 16, 2017.
7. publicbankinginstitute.org/intro_to_public_banking. Accessed May 7, 2017.
8. Bank of North Dakota Annual Report 2015.

9. ATB Financial 2016 Annual Report.
10. Bank of North Dakota Annual Report 2016.
11. ATB Financial 2017 Annual Report.
12. Statistics Canada, Cansim table 051-0005 (Estimates of Population, Canada, provinces, and territories).
13. census.gov/data/tables/2016/demo/popest/state-total.html. Accessed December 8, 2017.
14. aimco.alberta.ca/Who-We-Are/At-a-Glance.
15. Smart contracts are self-executing contracts with the terms of the agreement between buyer and seller being directly written into lines of code. The code and the agreements contained therein exist across a distributed, decentralized blockchain network. Smart contracts permit trusted transactions and agreements to be carried out among disparate, anonymous parties without the need for a central authority, legal system, or external enforcement mechanism. They render transactions traceable, transparent and irreversible. Source: Investopedia investopedia.com/terms/s/smart-contracts.asp#ixzz57PP5PUEY.

CHAPTER 11

Personal Well-Being

Well-being is a Choice

When asked about what they want out of life, most people respond, "I just want to be happy." I am often asked, How do you measure happiness? The answer is complicated.

John Lennon once reflected on his own happiness, noting, "When I was five years old, my mother always told me that happiness was the key to life. When I went to school, they asked me what I wanted to be when I grew up. I wrote down 'happy.' They told me I didn't understand the assignment, and I told them they didn't understand life."

There is no secret formula or recipe for a happy life. A fundamental question we all face in our lives is, Who am I and what am I here to accomplish?

Ten years of designing and testing well-being and happiness surveys in communities around the world has taught me that happiness is deeply personal and subjective. The response to a simple question such as "All things considered, how would you rate your life satisfaction?" yields interesting results. When you ask additional quality-of-life questions, such as perceptions of personal well-being, happiness, quality of sleep, spiritual well-being and sufficiency of income to meet life's needs, you get much richer insights into the complex nature of well-being. I would argue that well-being and happiness can be genuinely measured only through subjective surveys in which we ask people to self-rate their perceived well-being across many domains: happiness and hope; spiritual, mental, physical and emotional well-being; material/financial well-being; work-life balance; sense of belonging, trust and safety in communities; and feelings toward the natural environment.

My work is focused mainly on conducting well-being surveys in communities where individual and community well-being conditions can be assessed across various cohorts, including age, sex, income brackets, educational attainment, language, religion/spirituality and other socio-economic conditions. I'm currently conducting a well-being assessment for a community on the French Polynesian island of Tahiti. The early results point to interesting paradoxes: relatively moderate levels of life satisfaction (compared to the happier Nordic countries) yet very high levels of spiritual well-being. Despite relatively low levels of household income and a high proportion of survey respondents who feel their income is insufficient to meet life needs, Polynesians are content with their spiritual lives. While world happiness polls rank the Scandinavian countries, including Denmark, amongst top 10 happiest nations, they do not ask people to rate their spiritual well-being or the quality of their sleep. We are asking these questions in Tahiti to get a deeper appreciation of what makes life worthwhile in this South Pacific community that many of us perceive as paradise.

Is well-being an individual choice or a result of life circumstances? Or are we just genetically predisposed to a certain level of happiness? That depends on who you ask.

Earlier studies by some positive psychologists found that the key contributors to a happy life are the combination of the quality of one's upbringing and genetics (50%), followed by the strength and quality of relationships with family, friends and work colleagues (40%); a distant third is income and education (only 10%). I have learned that our subconscious mind is shaped by our life circumstances at home and our relationships with our parents and others between birth and age seven. We are profoundly shaped by what our parents told us and how we were socialized.

As we grow into adulthood we become more conscious of being human, but our lives and behaviors continue to be influenced by those earlier years. No matter how we strive to overcome some of the negative influences in our earlier life, we often seem incapable of transcending the earlier programming of our subconscious mind. Many adults spend their entire lifetime trying to overcome negative experiences or negative messaging from their parents, family and friends, even though their conscious minds aspire to greater happiness.

Most of us live our lives in the pursuit of inauthentic pleasures. We have few guides or teachers to help us orient our lives toward genuine happiness. Moreover, most of us aren't aware that the original Greek word for happiness is *eudaimonia*, which literally means the well-being of your spirit or soul.

In the indigenous traditions of the Cree people of Canada, spiritual well-being is just as important as physical, mental and emotional well-being. Cree elders believe that every child born is an answer to a prayer. What was the prayer of your grandparents or parents when you were born? What is your vocation, your calling in life? What are your real gifts, beyond what you have learned in school through hours of memorizing the knowledge your teachers attempted to input into your brain? Few of us ever delve deeply into our own souls and ask who we really are.

Positive psychologists and a few economists are developing a science of well-being, discovering the key ingredients for a happy and joyful life. Some of these ingredients seem obvious:

- a healthy and happy childhood;
- healthy and loving relationships with family;
- good food, health and physical exercise;
- friends and colleagues;
- strong sense of belonging to your community and neighborhood;
- trust;
- adequate income, relative to expectations, and;
- recreation time in the natural world.

Happiness economist John Helliwell of the University of British Columbia, along with Harvard University professor Robert Putnam (author of *Bowling Alone*), found evidence that confirms that social capital is strongly linked to subjective well-being through many independent channels and in several different forms. Marriage and family, ties to friends and neighbors, workplace ties, civic engagement (both individually and collectively), trustworthiness and trust: all appear independently and robustly related to happiness and life satisfaction, both directly and through their impact on health."[1]

In the *World Happiness Report* (2012) researchers report that, while genetics and environment are key features in determining a person's quality of life, there are other external features and personal features that contribute to a life of happiness or misery.[2] These known external features include

+ income;
+ work (being employed, with intrinsic motivation to work; eudemonic returns associated with flourishing; opportunities for advancement; job security; an interesting job; being allowed to work independently; the ability to help other people and be useful to society);
+ community and governance; and
+ values and religion.

Among the personal features that are key determinants of happiness are

+ mental health (mental illness constitutes 50% of total illness);
+ physical health (measured in terms of healthy life expectancy);
+ family experience (strength of family life measured by the proportion of people separated, divorced or widowed);
+ education (measured in terms of adult educational levels); and
+ gender and age (women tend to be less happy).

These external and personal features that are known to contribute most to happiness can become a framework for measuring and reporting well-being at any geographic scale. There is a two-way relationship between the factors that contribute to happiness and self-rated happiness. For example, health affects happiness and happiness affects health; there is a positive feedback relationship.

In a 2010 study of what contributed most to people's self-rated happiness in Victoria, British Columbia, epidemiologist Michael Pennock found the following top 12 issues (ranked from least to most important) of statistical importance:[3]

12. Who are very satisfied with their relationships with their friends

11. Who are very satisfied with their relationships with their family

10. Who are very satisfied with their ability to perform daily living activities

9. Who are very satisfied with their opportunity to develop skills and abilities

8. Who have a strong sense of belonging to their community

7. Who are very satisfied with their current job

6. Who are very satisfied with their ability to participate in community events—arts, culture, recreations and sports

5. Who report their health status as excellent

4. Who report their mental health as excellent

3. Who are very satisfied with their health

2. Whose lives are not at all stressful

1. Who spend all their time doing things they enjoy

Because these 12 factors are strongly correlated with perceived life satisfaction and happiness, we can be relatively confident that asking questions about them will give us a fairly robust barometer of individual and community well-being.

This list suggests that we have direct control over most aspects of our lives. We can now self-assess our own lives through the lens of these happiness criteria and identify areas in which we would like to improve our lives.

Money, Your Life and Happiness

There is a long-standing debate about whether money buys happiness. Some argue that money cannot buy happiness. Some researchers have found that there may be a threshold of income and self-rated happiness, somewhere around $70,000 per household. Yet others would disagree, arguing that incremental increases in income secure marginally more happiness. I'm not sure there will ever be an objective way of measuring the sufficiency of income or money relative to life needs. More often than not, most of us live life wanting more stuff and thus more money. This may vary over time and diminish as we age. For some, there can never be enough money.

If there is no objective measure of an optimum level of money and well-being, perhaps we need to rely on perceptions instead. In the well-being surveys I've conducted, I ask people how they feel about the sufficiency of income or money and life satisfaction. The question is, Do you feel your current level of income is sufficient to meet your life needs? I have found that only about 30%–35% of a population feel their income is insufficient to meet their needs. It turns out that this is often identical to my estimates of the percentage of the population who is not earning a living wage—enough income to participate fully in an economy or society.

Recent studies of happiness and money suggest that more money increases your well-being only if you spend it on the right things. Research by Harvard Business School has found that spending more money on buying more free time by hiring a cook or house cleaner increases a person's perceived well-being, while spending more money on material possessions does little to improve happiness.[4] The researchers (including Dr. Ashley Whillans at Harvard Business School and Elizabeth Dunn from the University of British Columbia) surveyed more than 6,000 adults in the United States, Denmark, Canada and the Netherlands. They found that "people who hire a housecleaner or pay the kid next door to mow the lawn might feel like they're being lazy. But our results suggest that buying time has similar benefits for happiness as having more money."

In my own life I have experienced the benefits of having more free time to pursue things I enjoy, including writing books or spending time mentoring a young business person or social entrepreneur. Too often we lament not having enough time to pursue the things that might make us happier.

One of the most important contributors to my own well-being and happiness has been my relationship with money. You can tell that I have spent my professional lifetime examining the nature of money and our relationship with it. Money may be only a social invention that we have created out of our imagination to serve as a tool for exchange of goods and time in our economy, but it has one of the most mysterious and profound influences on our lives. We cannot live without money. We say "we make money," when in fact banks create money as the life-blood for our lives. We exchange our time through work for money so we can buy the things in life that we hope will make us happy. We never seem to have enough money, or rather never *feel* we have enough money. We know in our hearts that money will not buy us happiness, yet we buy lottery tickets hoping to get rich quick. On our deathbeds we are unlikely to use our last breath telling those we love how much money we made.

One of the most important books I have ever read is *Your Money or Your Life* by Vicki Robbins and Joe Dominguez (1999). It profoundly changed my understanding of time and money. I realized that each moment in our lives is a choice of how we will spend the most precious of all things, time. We choose how we spend the roughly 740,000 hours we have to live from birth to death (with an average life expectancy of 84+ years). We spend a good portion of that time sleeping and a large portion of our waking hours working for money.

Each day we give up some of our time for money. Some argue that most of us are not "making a living" but "making a dying." Certainly those of us who are mortgaged would agree. For most of us there seems to be no choice between money and our lives.

Making money and stressing about our debts and how we will pay the bills dominates our waking hours; life is what we fit into the few remaining hours in the day.

In my own experience as a small business owner and economic consultant, I have learned the precious value of discretionary time. I've had to learn how to balance the need to make sufficient income from my economic consultancy with the discretionary time I chose to spend with family, friends, in nature and mentoring others. I experienced the joy of having extra time once all of our financial debts (mortgages, car loans, credit card balances) were paid in full. When my wife and I had paid off our mortgage and found ourselves with more discretionary income, we had the choice of either working less for money or spending our new discretionary income on a bigger house or more material things. We opted to enjoy our first and only home, maintain our current possessions, live relatively frugally and enjoy more discretionary lifetime energy on our children and with family and neighbors. In many ways I experienced the same positive well-being impacts (i.e., more free time) as those in the Harvard study. We paid ourselves in terms of more discretionary time.

I've learned that there is great freedom and joy in living unencumbered by financial debts. Spending less of our earned income on interest payments means we have more time to dedicate to the things that bring life joy and greater personal and family well-being. I envision a world where we all may experience the joy of more free time, less debt, and thus greater well-being.

Notes

1. John F. Helliwell and Robert Putnam. "The social context of well-being." *Phil. Trans. R. Soc. Lond. B* (2004) 359, 1435–1446 1435 # 2004 The Royal Society doi:10.1098/rstb.2004.1522.
2. *World Happiness Report*. 2012. Edited by John Helliwell, Richard Layard and Jeffrey Sachs. 2012, p. 59.
3. *Greater Victoria Wellbeing Survey 2010*. Happiness Index Partnership and the Victoria Foundation. Study conducted by Michael Pennock.
4. telegraph.co.uk/science/2017/07/24/money-really-can-buy-happiness -say-scientists/.

Epilogue

BUILDING THE NEW ECONOMY of well-being represents one of the most important new economic paradigm shifts of our time, at a time when the world most needs an alternative to the current financial and economic malaise.

If well-being and quality of life are not the highest aspirations for an economy, then what was the economy designed for? Is not the purpose of our lives, both individually and collectively, to pursue a life of meaning, joy and love? The quest for well-being has always been our most important goal.

An economy of well-being is a common-sense approach to economics, accounting and finance that builds on the best attributes and tools from these professions while replacing the dominant financial measures of progress and success with the more compelling measures of well-being, happiness and joy. We might describe a well-being economy with the following words: caring, sharing, sense of belonging, compassion, love for place and others, joy and an appreciation for the gifts of abundance that Mother Nature provides us every day.

An economy is the most important decision-making system in our societies. It is a thing we have created (like a game) whose rules we can change at any time. While the pursuit of well-being is ultimately an individual choice, a society can collectively orient itself toward the highest possible state of well-being for both people and nature. Indeed, the purpose of an economy should

211

be to enable the conditions in which all people can achieve the highest possible subjective states of well-being. Building a new economy based on well-being is compelling because it is what most of us ultimately want from life.

A well-being economy will be built on a solid foundation of the emerging science of well-being. Studies by psychologists and happiness economists are showing that well-being can be measured. Individuals, communities and businesses that experience healthy and trusting relationships, are active in their communities and live in a flourishing natural environment will live longer and more fulfilling lives and enjoy high levels of self-rated well-being. The social and physical climate of a community is a better predictor of well-being than income or changes in GDP growth. Ultimately, a well-being economy and society is more resilient to life's shocks.

Having just returned from measuring well-being in Tahiti, I can attest to a common yearning amongst all people for a life that is rich in well-being, relationships and a harmonious relationship with Mother Nature. I was honored to assist the Tahitian initiative *Te aroha ia rahi* ("May our love flourish"). My hope is that this initiative, from the same South Pacific island that British Captain James Cook called "the island of love" after his visit in 1769, will be the catalyst for a global shift toward a new economic paradigm based on well-being, happiness, beauty and what the French call extreme *bonheur* (or bliss).

Whether in our own lives, our families, our neighborhoods, our workplaces or in our towns, cities, states, provinces or nations, there are immediate steps we can take toward building this new economy. This begins with measuring what matters to our individual and collective well-being by asking the most intuitive question of all: How do you feel about your life? Another key question is, How much material and financial wealth do I/my family need to live a life of comfort and sufficiency? Our individual and collective responses to these two fundamental questions are the ultimate measure of society's progress.

As with all journeys, we must first envision the future, create a map for the journey, take the right gear and venture forth knowing that there will be obstacles and challenges, detours and potholes, successes and disappointments. Yet just like Dorothy in the *Wizard of Oz*, when she set out down the Yellow Brick Road, we may be pleasantly surprised at what we learn about ourselves, each other and the hope we experience, confident that we have the heart, mind and courage to accomplish what may seem impossible.

Just as in the design and building of a house, an economy of well-being will require a clear vision of what it will look like, how it will function, how we will govern it, and how we will feel once we have constructed the new economic model and lived in it for some time. It is said that the devil is in the details. Notwithstanding, the path and the details will present themselves as we walk the path and build the new economy.

I hope my book inspires you and your friends and colleagues with practical ideas and tools to start your own journey toward enduring well-being and genuine joy in your life, your family, your workplace and your community.

En-Joy the journey!

Index

About the Author

MARK ANIELSKI is an economic strategist specializing in the economics of well-being. He is schooled in ecological economics, accounting and forestry. He has advised nations and communities in Canada, Bhutan, French Polynesia (Tahiti), The Netherlands, Austria and China in their aspirations to develop a new economic model based on well-being and happiness. He is the author of the award-winning book *The Economics of Happiness: Building Genuine Wealth*, which provides a blueprint for building the new economy of well-being. In 2008 *Alberta Venture* magazine named him one of Alberta's 50 most influential people. Mark was recently named to the Province of Alberta's Audit Committee, which reviews the Government of Alberta's financial and annual reports. He is an international expert in natural capital accounting and recently co-founded the Centre for Integral Finance and Economics (London, UK) that focuses on developing new tools to support the emerging field of impact investment and banking.

ABOUT NEW SOCIETY PUBLISHERS

New Society Publishers is an activist, solutions-oriented publisher focused on publishing books for a world of change. Our books offer tips, tools, and insights from leading experts in sustainable building, homesteading, climate change, environment, conscientious commerce, renewable energy, and more—positive solutions for troubled times.

We're proud to hold to the highest environmental and social standards of any publisher in North America. This is why some of our books might cost a little more. We think it's worth it!

- We print all our books in North America, never overseas

- All our books are printed on **100% post-consumer recycled paper**, processed chlorine-free, with low-VOC vegetable-based inks (since 2002)

- Our corporate structure is an innovative employee shareholder agreement, so we're one-third employee-owned (since 2015)

- We're carbon-neutral (since 2006)

- We're certified as a B Corporation (since 2016)

At New Society Publishers, we care deeply about *what* we publish—but also about *how* we do business.

Download our catalogue at https://newsociety.com/Our-Catalog or for a printed copy please email info@newsocietypub.com or call 1-800-567-6772 ext 111.

New Society Publishers
ENVIRONMENTAL BENEFITS STATEMENT

For every 5,000 books printed, New Society saves the following resources:[1]

25	Trees
2,264	Pounds of Solid Waste
2,491	Gallons of Water
3,249	Kilowatt Hours of Electricity
4,115	Pounds of Greenhouse Gases
18	Pounds of HAPs, VOCs, and AOX Combined
6	Cubic Yards of Landfill Space

[1] Environmental benefits are calculated based on research done by the Environmental Defense Fund and other members of the Paper Task Force who study the environmental impacts of the paper industry.

MIX
Paper from responsible sources
FSC® C016245
www.fsc.org

www.newsociety.com